Cambridge Elements

Elements in Theatre, Performance and the Political
edited by
Trish Reid
University of Reading
Liz Tomlin
University of Glasgow

PERFORMING NATIONALISM IN RUSSIA

Yana Meerzon
University of Ottawa

Shaftesbury Road, Cambridge CB2 8EA, United Kingdom

One Liberty Plaza, 20th Floor, New York, NY 10006, USA

477 Williamstown Road, Port Melbourne, VIC 3207, Australia

314–321, 3rd Floor, Plot 3, Splendor Forum, Jasola District Centre, New Delhi – 110025, India

103 Penang Road, #05–06/07, Visioncrest Commercial, Singapore 238467

Cambridge University Press is part of Cambridge University Press & Assessment, a department of the University of Cambridge.

We share the University's mission to contribute to society through the pursuit of education, learning and research at the highest international levels of excellence.

www.cambridge.org
Information on this title: www.cambridge.org/9781009451932

DOIs: 10.1017/9781009451949

When citing this work, please include a reference to the DOIs 10.1017/9781009451949

First published 2024

A catalogue record for this publication is available from the British Library

ISBN 978-1-009-45193-2 Hardback
ISBN 978-1-009-45196-3 Paperback
ISSN 2753-1244 (online)
ISSN 2753-1236 (print)

Performing Nationalism in Russia

Elements in Theatre, Performance and the Political

DOIs: 10.1017/9781009451949
First published online: February 2024

Yana Meerzon
University of Ottawa

Author for correspondence: Yana Meerzon, ymeerzon@uottawa.ca

Abstract: Following Homi Bhabha's prompt on reading nationalism as a set of discursive and performative practices, this Element focuses on the cultural geography of today's Russia and examines a range of performative strategies used by the Russian state to uphold its nationalist project. Simultaneously, it maps artistic strategies of resistance to the ideology of nationalism as employed by both state-funded and independent theatre companies, via new dramaturgies, performance practices, and strategies of storytelling.

Keywords: nationalism, political performance, Putin's Russia, cultural resistance, performances of protest

ISBNs: 9781009451932 (HB), 9781009451963 (PB), 9781009451949 (OC)
ISSNs: 2753-1244 (online), 2753-1236 (print)

Contents

Introduction: What Is Russian Nationalism?

Nationalism is a relatively new concept. In Europe, it originated in the aftermath of the philosophical project of the Enlightenment. Historically, it has taken many forms – ethnic, religious, territorial, cultural, linguistic, affective, and banal – all of which have a substantial literature. It contributed to nation-building processes based on remapping territories, colonialism, totalitarianism, and regionalism. In its more recent forms, it has been redefined as a civic project rooted in the ground of multiculturalism or conceptualized as an 'imagined political community' (Anderson, 1991:6). At the time of writing, nations increasingly respond to environmental, political, global, and military crises by turning to discourses and practices of nationalism. Leaders appeal directly to the populist and tribal instincts of their peoples. In opposition to individual freedoms and human rights, this nationalism is exclusively and explicitly about borders – physical and otherwise. It appeals 'to the rich and the powerful', but also to citizens threatened by the disappearing homogeneity of the collective 'we' (Bull, 2018:8). Redefining nationalism and highlighting its dangers have become vital to political performance and activism and thus constitute conceptual focal points of this Element.

Russia presents a compelling case study for the examination of contemporary nationalism(s) because in Russia, nationalism has long been tightly connected with the nation-building process. In Russia, the nation-building dates to the reforms of Peter the Great (1672–1725) and has evolved through the age of industrialization and the social upheavals of the twentieth century. Since the collapse of the Soviet Union in 1991, the country has experienced a series of radical changes. After a period of so-called liberalization, it witnessed the return of state-controlled economic and cultural policies under Vladimir Putin, who has served continually as president or prime minister since 2000. The 2020 Russian constitution formalizes these shifts. It recognizes ethnic Russians as the nation-forming people and Russian as the country's official language. It solidifies Putin's search for a 'unified national idea', which he began in the early 2000s. This idea emphasizes Orthodox Christianity, heterosexual marriage (so-called traditional values), strong borders, patriotism, loyalty, and a Russia-centric representation of history. These values constitute a foundation of the nation-building processes in Putin's Russia, which has been based on the slowly evolving mechanisms of oppression and censorship, or what Lev Gudkov calls Russia's '*vozvratniy ili vtorichniy*'/'recurring or secondary' totalitarianism (Gudkov, 2018:255–7). In this Element, I use the terms 'nationalism in Russia' and 'Russian nationalism' interchangeably.

When Russia began its unlawful invasion of Ukraine in February 2022, many Russian citizens took to the streets to protest the actions of their government.

The regime responded immediately by shutting down independent media and artistic expression and by arresting individuals. On 4 March 2022, the Federal Assembly passed a series of amendments to the Criminal Code of the Russian Federation, seeking administrative and criminal responsibility for the dissemination of misinformation (called 'fakes' in Russian) about the Russian Armed Forces (The State Duma, 2022a). Substantial fines, criminal charges, and imprisonment for up to ten years were listed as potential punishments.

This Element reflects this moment of catastrophe and documents the performative practices of nationalism and resistances to it that have been building in Putin's Russia. The war in Ukraine has only intensified what has been developing in the country in the past two decades. Contemporary Russia is hostage to propaganda, partisan interpretations of its own history, and general political passivity. While acknowledging the devastating impact of Russia's war on Ukraine and its people, my focus is on the terrible outcomes of the invasion on the home front, with Putin's government turning its war machine against its own people.

The work of theatre artists chosen for this Element supports the following argument: as it has been censored, prohibited, and eventually closed, with its creators silenced, put under arrest, or forced into exile, this work exemplifies the dire state of political theatre in Russia. What was somewhat possible during the past two decades has come to an end today, yet the sheer existence of the art as protest provides hope and what Russians call 'a breath of fresh air' under dictatorship, and thus can be studied as an act of resistance to the homogenizing narratives and performances of nationalism.

Structure

Theatre and performance occupy a special place in the hierarchy of devices used by the state to advance its nationalist agenda and also by artists to resist it. State-endorsed performances of nationalism include the justice and penal systems, but also state-sponsored media and televised events, mass commemorations and celebrations, military and sports parades, pop music concerts, and other cultural events. These examples constitute a necessary point of departure, a kind of artistic and ideological reference point, to identify the emotional and affectual anchors of Russian nationalism. Section 1 analyses these instances of the performance of nationalism, including Putin's personal televised theatrics. Silencing through censorship, loss of employment, public ostracism, political and physical persecution, imprisonment, and exile are among the potential outcomes that await artists who decide to question the country's nationalist agenda or to tackle difficult sociopolitical issues in artistic language not fully endorsed by the regime. In Section 2, I begin to study how Russian theatre artists subvert the authoritarian discourses of nationalism. The aim is to unpack the uneasy interdependence between state and artist to demonstrate that when theatre-making depends on state funding, artists, specifically politically mindful ones, are often forced to compromise between personal aspirations and state expectations. I use the widely known case of Kirill Serebrennikov, the former artistic director of the Gogol Centre in Moscow, who was put on trial on allegations of financial fraud, to exemplify this difficult artist versus state interdependency. In Section 3, I use Olga Malinova's work on symbolic politics, 'Politika pamyati kak oblast' simvolicheskoy politiki' (Malinova, 2018), to explore Anastasia Patlay and Nana Grinstein's documentary theatre, which brings historical documents and figures on stage. Their 2022 project *Memoria*, which interweaves three historical narratives of oppression as mobilized by the authoritarian state, demonstrates that by contrasting newly discovered accounts of the past with the glorified narratives of official history, documentary theatre can resist the homogenizing narratives of nationalism. Section 4 examines the figure of the other and the binary of exclusion and inclusion, which forms the basis of nationalism. It uses and applies methodologies of 'decolonial aestheSis' (Tlostanova, 2019) as strategies of resistance to nationalism's performative discourses and practices. My focus here is on the work of post-Soviet racialized artists, who use theatre to stage multiple cultural, ethnic, linguistic, and religious belongings. I begin with Nuria Fatykhova's project *Avazlar/Voices* (2020–1) produced by Theatre Platform MOÑ (Kazan), which aims to resurrect the Tatar language through participatory performance, and in so doing contests the colonizing narratives and practices of Russian nationalism.

With the war raging in Ukraine, which further solidified nation-building sentiment there, calls for decolonization, both in practice and as a scholarly framework to better understand Russia's imperial history, have gained momentum.[1] In this Element, I follow Alexander Etkind's injunction to read Russia's colonial practices as a 'dialectic in standstill' (Etkind, 2011:2). Historically, Russia expanded its military, economic, and cultural influence by annexing neighbouring countries to its west, such as Poland through its several partitions, and, at the same time, by developing its previously colonized eastern territories: what Etkind calls self- or internal colonization (2). Thus, 'Russia has

[1] Among recent publications on this topic see *Canadian Slavonic Papers* (65:2; 2023) and the 2023 annual convention of the Association for Slavic, East European, & Eurasian Studies, fully dedicated to the theme 'Decolonization' (www.aseees.org/convention/2023-aseees-convention-theme).

been both the subject and the object of colonization and its corollaries, such as orientalism' (2). Studying resistance to this type of colonization, as Mladina Tlostanova notes, requires 'destabilizing the usual subject-object relationship from a specific position of those who have been denied subjectivity and rationality and regarded as mere tokens of their culture, religion, sexuality, race, and gender' (Tlostanova, 2015:40). Its key strategy, to which Fatykhova's work is dedicated, is creating 'epistemic subjects and looking at the world from the position of our own origins, lived experiences, and education' (40).

In my second example, I spotlight the nexus of migration and nationalism. Migration – internal and external – has presented a particular challenge for the development of post-Soviet Russia. With the collapse of the Soviet Union and Russia's borders opening to the outside world, emigration caused a serious outflow of intellectual and creative power from the country. On the other hand, internal migration – mostly from central to eastern and northern regions of the country and from rural to urban areas – posed ethnocultural, social, and demographic challenges, which precipitated changes in government policy. The Kazakh-Russian writer Olzhas Zhanaidarov brings historical and contemporary Kazakh characters, often migrants from Kazakhstan to Russia, to the Russian stage. In his plays *Dzhut* (2013), which is dedicated to the memory of the famine in 1930s Soviet Kazakhstan, and *Magazin/Store* (2015), which describes the slave-like existence of female Kazakh migrant workers in Moscow, Zhanaidarov not only questions myths of equality and diversity as mobilized by Putin's propaganda, but also invites a racialized migrant – the proverbial *stranger-danger* (Ahmed, 2000:24) – into the theatrical spotlight, and so demonstrates that in today's Russia, oppressive cultural and legislative structures work to reproduce the repressive social, familial, and gender practices of migrants.

In my Conclusion, I revisit the notion of nationalism as a powerful but dangerous sociopolitical construct that can be promoted or resisted through the arts. My closing example is the so-called second theatre trial – the first being the case of Serebrennikov – which began on 4 May 2023, when the theatre director Zhenya (Evgeniya) Berkovich and the playwright Svetlana Petriichuk were arrested on suspicion of supporting terrorism in their award-winning 2020 production, *Finist Yasniy Sokol/Finist the Brave Falcon*. The case is ongoing, with the trial set for January 2024. This is the first criminal case in Russia in which an artistic work has triggered political persecution and criminal charges. It signifies the increasingly punitive character of Russian censorship. It is also no coincidence that a play about the abuse of women has been targeted. Preservation of the patriarchy and its values is a key nation-building strategy, as evidenced by the Presidential Decree N 809, *On Approval of the*

Fundamentals of State Policy to Preserve and Strengthen Traditional Russian Spiritual and Moral Values (The State Duma, 2022c). Effectively, this case targets not simply two female artists but their feminist position.

Nationalism and the Russian Context

Whether as a theoretical concept, historical phenomenon, or political and legislative practice, nationalism is multifaceted and difficult to define. It can be understood as a type of ideology, but also 'as a social movement and symbolic language', and as a cultural practice that has multiple 'meanings, varieties and sources' (Smith, 2001:1). Inevitably, studying nationalism 'entails a consideration of related concepts, such as the nation, national identity and the national state' (1). In an 1882 lecture, the French orientalist Ernest Renan formulated basic principles of the idea of nation as a man-made construct, but also as 'a spiritual principle, the outcome of the profound complications of history', and 'a spiritual family' of independent subjects, 'not a group determined by the shape of the earth' (Renan, 1990:18–19). Resting on principles of simultaneity, the nation is a living organism that thinks of itself in several temporal dimensions: the past, with its glorious, traumatic, embarrassing, and hopeful legacies; the present, defined by peoples' desire or resistance to living together; and a set of collective aspirations for the future. For Renan, a nation has no right of possession of people or territories. Free individuals come together as a group to produce a 'kind of moral conscience which we call a nation' (20). Not everyone agrees with this analysis.

More recently, Ronald Suny has defined the nation as a 'group of people that imagines itself to be a political community that is distinct from the rest of humankind, believes that it shares characteristics, perhaps origins, values, historical experiences, language, territory' (Suny, 2001:28). Crucially, based on its shared culture, this nation 'deserves self-determination' and consequently lays claim to 'territory (the "homeland") and a state' (28). Moreover, Suny observes, nations are 'the result of the hard constitutive intellectual and political work of elites and masses' (28). This work mobilizes the nation's understanding of its collective history, rooted in the individual stories of its citizens. Since the late eighteenth century, European nations have sought more concrete forms of self-identification. In many cases, 'the state merged with the "nation" to claim its new status as a nation-state' (28). This process of self-identification involved 'ethnicised communities' seeking recognition as 'cultural communit[ies] of shared language, religion, and/or other characteristics with a durable, antique past, shared kinship, common origins, and narratives of progress through time' (28).

The theatre scholar Nadine Holdsworth echoes some of these ideas. For Holdsworth, the nation is 'one of the most powerful markers of identity and belonging' upon which rests four foundational principles (Holdsworth, 2010:9). The first is the idea of the nation as a territorial community marked by clear borders. Secondly, language identifies the nation as a regulated community, although the official language(s) of the state can be different to that of the family. Heredity and ethnic belonging constitute the third principle. Most relevant to my aims in this Element is the fourth principle, the nation as defined by cultural output. This includes, for instance, the invention of national literature, drama, and theatre, both as constituent elements in education and culture, and also as ideological platforms. Systems of state governance, cultural institutions, and individual artists participate in making and dismantling images of the nation. They mobilize ideological and affectual mechanisms in performing nationalism.

For the political historian Eric Hobsbawm, nationalism is an emotional phenomenon, often manifesting as patriotism, as the expression of peoples' loyalty to the place of belonging and their willingness to 'identify themselves emotionally with "their" nation and to be politically mobilised as Czechs, Germans, Italians' (Hobsbawm, 1989:143). The desire to belong can be 'politically exploited', however, and nationalism can be mobilized for progress or for tyranny and colonization (143). Because of its constructed nature, nationalism and its ideologies, assumptions, and sentiments can be easily manipulated. Benedict Anderson famously described the nation as 'an imagined political community' (Anderson, 1991:6). For him, 'nation-ness' is 'a cultural artifact of a particular kind', which claims a special 'emotional legacy' on its members even if those members 'will never know most of their fellow-members' (4). In Anderson's view, the nation is defined by its semiotic and affectual systems of belonging because it is in the minds of its members that 'the image of their communion' lives (6). Anderson's notion of the nation as an imagined community 'extends Renan's appeal to collectivity and an interconnected national moral conscience' (20). 'Conceived as a deep, horizontal comradeship', this trope connects the experiences of the individuals to those of the group (7).

The recent resurgence of nationalist aspirations in Europe is typically led by conservatives and is accompanied by aggression against individual freedoms and human rights, nostalgia for the colonial project, and fear of the (racialized) other. Characterized by authoritarian systems of government, which capitalize on village psychology, today's nationalisms mobilize the rhetoric of populism, and in so doing expose the dangers of nationalist rhetoric (Sennett, 2011:49).

In Russia, nationalism has long been tightly connected to the nation-building process, which historians identify either as 'the question of nation' or a state (Suny, 2001:35). Its practices and narratives evolved through expansion of territories and colonization of both the neighbouring peoples and the ethnic groups settled within Russian borders. From 988, when Orthodox Christianity was adopted as the state religion, the Church played a special role in defining Russia as a nation by fusing 'the notions of Orthodoxy and Russianness' (35). At the time, conversion to Orthodox Christianity allowed individuals to fully 'assimilate into the Russian community' (36). For centuries, however, and depending on the region, integration of the colonized people varied: often, 'peasant or nomadic populations . . . retained their tribal, ethnic, and religious identities. Some elites, like the Tatar and Ukrainian nobles, dissolved into the Russian *dvoriantsvo* (nobility), but others, like the German barons of the Baltic or the Swedish aristocrats of Finland, retained privileges and separate identities' (41). From the mid-nineteenth century till the Bolshevik Revolution in 1917, there were two complementary practices of assimilation into the empire for non-ethnic Russians – 'Russification' and 'Russianization'. The first one presupposed 'a surrender of ethnic identity through forced assimilation'; the second 'mean[t] the increased hegemony of Russian language, culture, and institutions' (Pearson, 1989:89). By implementing these practices, the authorities bolstered 'the empire's polyethnic borderlands' and 'ensure[d] the political loyalty and social stability' of non-dominant national groups (Staliūnas, 2007:7). As a result, ethnic minorities were gradually losing their territories, religious and cultural identities, and languages while ethnic Russians grew stronger as the leading group of the empire (Pearson, 1989:94). By the early twentieth century, ethnic groups' resistance to losing their privileges had significantly grown. To a certain degree, it was the unrest of the minorities that instigated the 1905 Russian Revolution. To prevent this revolution from spreading across the empire, Nicolas II made compromises to the Russification policy. The freedoms did not last for too long: the new administration, headed by Peter Stolypin, 'returned to Russification with a heightened sense of urgency and renewed vigor' (99). By the time the Bolsheviks came to power, the empire had successfully reimplemented its nationality policy, and so it prepared a fruitful soil for the ethnic groups' further assimilation and acculturation to take place during the Soviet period. After the Bolsheviks turned the Russian empire into the Soviet empire, many pre-1917 patterns of nation-building made a comeback. In the 1930s, Stalin personally supported the rebirth of Russian nationalism. He 'took a keen interest in research on Slavic antiquity and hoped that such research would help the Soviet regime demonstrate the primeval communism of Russians' (Laruelle, 2019:75). Communism was a convenient doctrine for Soviet nationalists and under their influence it functioned as a new religion in uniting the peoples of the USSR. Moreover, as Marlene Laruelle notes, from 'the mid-1960s, some state and party organs . . . undertook a discreet attempt to fuse Soviet ideology and Russian nationalism, progressively rehabilitating both

Orthodoxy and neo-paganism' (75). The myth of internationalism, the equality of all workers living in and beyond the USSR, was another strong trope of Soviet nationalism. The slogan 'Friendship of the Peoples' reflected the unity of Soviet citizens with each other and against external enemies. With the benefit of hindsight, we can see that Mikhail Gorbachev's top-down reforms and democratization of the Soviet systems of political, cultural, and economic control made the collapse of the Soviet empire inevitable. As Suny observes, the 'implosion of the center allowed the subordinate peripheries' to seek their independence (Suny, 2001:33). Many former Soviet republics, from Ukraine to Georgia, and autonomic regions within Russia itself, like Tatarstan or Bashkiria, embarked on the road of national self-determination and decoloniality.

In the summer of 1996, after his re-election as Russia's president, Boris Yeltsin called on his compatriots to come up with a new national idea, something 'to rival the American Dream' and to help people 'erase all memories of Glory to the Communist Party of the Soviet Union' (Rubin, 1996). This call was issued through the government-supported *Rossiyskaya Gazeta*, which offered a prize of $2,000 for the best entry. Suggestions ranged from reviving the Russian spirit with the help of the Russian Orthodox Church to asking each Russian citizen to 'take personal responsibility for the country's future' (Rubin, 1996). However, in the country that had just freed itself from the seventy-year grip of one ideology, there was no appetite for embracing another, and Yeltsin's admittedly ludicrous experiment failed. At the same time, nationalism experienced a surge in the USSR's former republics, which were now actively seeking territorial, political, cultural, and economic independence. 'Baltic nationalisms', as Laruelle observes, 'and, to a lesser extent, their Ukrainian, Moldovan, and Georgian counterparts were praised for contributing to the democratization of their republics and their engagement with the West, while their ethnocentric "excesses" were excused as corollaries to a necessary phase of national political construction' (Laruelle, 2019:3). In response, Yeltsin opted for a pluralist concept 'Rossiyane'/ 'Russian citizens' as 'Moscow's answer to the nationalism of the ethnic republics' (3).

With Putin coming to power, Russian nation-building returned. It capitalized on people's nostalgia for the Soviet past and on Putin's personal conviction that the collapse of the USSR was one of the major historical catastrophes of the twentieth century. Putin's position sharply contrasted with Yeltsin's, which was to represent the end of the USSR as consistent with historical trends and hence 'progressive, even if difficult' (Malinova, 2018:95). The difference was obvious from the start. In his presidential address to the Federal Assembly in July 2000, a newly elected President Putin called for 'a resurrection of patriotism and historical memory as a means to reinforce national unity' (Wood, 2011:177).

Revising the nation's history via the figure of the Father of the Nation standing above his people in the performative posture of the saviour of the Motherland was to be Putin's strategy. 'Putin and his handlers have structured his rule from the outset as a performance' and have aspired to create an image of power and protection which aligns Putin personally 'with the fate of the country' (173). This protector narrative – legitimized in the 2020 constitutional reforms – was based on such traditional Russian values as the hetero-normal family, patriarchy, and Orthodox Christianity. It promised to observe and defend Russia's strong borders and its military power, and to recognize ethnic Russians as a nation-forming group. In addition, the protector narrative placed Putin at the centre of this myth-making process, which reinforced connections between the country's past, present, and future. For example, the Kremlin ideologists purposefully deployed World War II – 'an event of mythic proportions that underlines the unity and coherence of the nation, gives it legitimacy and status as a world power' – in their propaganda (174). Constructed during the Soviet time and revived in Putin's ideological program, the myth of the Great Patriotic War – 'simultaneously timeless and rooted in time, that involves suffering and redemption, trauma and recovery from the trauma' – was mobilized by the Kremlin propagandists to better define Russia's identity, rationale, and purpose (174). This manipulation of history in combination with the creation of new political myths, convenient for the regime and its oppressive policies, constitutes what Olga Malinova calls a 'politics of cultural memory', which, unlike professional historiography, operates with 'simplified narratives that reduce complex and contradictory historical processes to convenient and emotionally coloured schemes' (Malinova, 2018:37). Today's idealogues of Russian nationalism continue to build on these narratives and myths. They present Russian history – from the Battle of the Neva (1240) to Napoleon's invasion (1812) and now the war in Ukraine – as cyclical, always in confrontation with the collective West, continually fighting its enemies for political, cultural, and economic independence. In this model, Russia does not lose, so it must mobilize all its structures and institutions, including the church, as means to guarantee imminent success.

According to Laruelle, there are four trends of Russian nationalism as it developed under Putin's regime: Imperial nationalism, Eastern Slavic nationalism, Ethnic Russian nationalism, and '*Rossiiskii* nationalism', which presupposes 'a visa regime with Central Asia and the Caucasus and a specific status for ethnic Russians inside Russia, but with no support for Russian irredentism in the "near abroad"' (Laruelle, 2019:7). To reinforce these trends, Putin's propaganda machine utilizes the emotional energies of his supporters, which include his own administration and multiple conservative forces. Although Putin's presidential office cultivates an image of a pluralist ideological apparatus from which the state's philosophical doctrine stems, his most loyal and powerful group of supporters is comprised of the ambitious state apparatchiks, who are the successors of the last generation of the Soviet managerial elite, and who dream of using their access to power to change Russia. They support Putin's nationalist project because it is so firmly rooted in 'coercion and violence as methods of governance and ways of self-preservation' (Pastukhov, 2022). The second influential group of Putin's supporters consists of a powerful political, ideological, and spiritual conglomerate of individuals interconnected by ideas of national Bolshevism, conservative patriotism, and fascism. This group includes Russian Eurasians like Alexander Dugin, Russian Fascists – followers of Ivan Ilyin's philosophical teachings – and Communists, among others. Because they do not hold influential administrative positions, for this group, violence is an end in itself and it has no limitations. For the Kremlin apparatchiks, however, violence, even war, is only an instrument for retaining power (Pastukhov, 2022). Putin serves as connecting tissue between the rationalism of Kremlin's apparatchiks and the irrationalism of the other group.

The conceptual construct of the 'Russian World' is the cornerstone to these ideologies. It is based on philosophies and practices of (self)-isolationism and colonization which seek to impose a special way of being on the Russian diaspora worldwide and the country's closest neighbours. Formulated by Petr Shchedrovitsky in the article 'Russkiy mir i transnatsional'noe russkoe' (2000), the Russian World mobilizes a form of ethnic nationalism rooted in the supremacy of the Russian language. To Shchedrovitsky, 'those who speak Russian in their everyday life – also *think* Russian, and as a result – *act* Russian' (Kudors, 2010:3). They deserve protection both within the borders of Russia itself and worldwide. Since Putin's coming to power, this ambiguous ideological concept has been institutionalized and promoted. In 2007, Putin signed a decree to establish the Russian World Foundation. Supported through state funds and designed on similar principles to the British Council or the Goethe Institute, this foundation was intended to work in tandem with the Russian Orthodox Church to promote the Russian language and Russian culture worldwide, so to make the Russian World the keystone of the country's global influence and soft power (3). Metropolitan Kirill, the leader of the Russian Orthodox Church, supported the Russian World idea. In 2006, he declared that 'a unique Russian civilization, consisting of Russia and the Russian World, should oppose Western civilization in its assertion of the universality of the Western tradition' (3). Such rhetoric prepared the ideological ground for the annexation of Ukrainian territories and the 2022 war.

The far-right political philosopher Alexander Dugin's geopolitical theory of neo-Eurasianism dovetails with the notion of the Russian World. Influenced by Western right-wing intellectuals, teachings of the anthropologist Lev Gumilev, and Russian national-patriotic ideologies, Dugin's philosophical doctrine promotes 'conspiracy theories of the forthcoming "final war" (*Endkampf*) between the "Eurasian" and "Atlanticist orders"' (Shekhovtsov, 2015:40). His neo-Eurasianism relies on the view of Russia as the Third Continent between Europe and Asia, called to enact a special 'Third Way between capitalism and communism' (Laruelle, 2015:11). This doctrine is openly 'anti-Western, anti-Transatlantic, and anti-liberal, and it believes in the common destiny of European and Eurasian peoples' (11). The Kremlin has never openly aligned itself with Dugin. However, the European far right, including Arktos, the publishing house of the British New Right, Mateusz Piskorski (former Polish MP and 'head of the small think tank European Center for Geopolitical Analysis'), as well as Dugin's friends in Greece and Turkey (15), share this 'anti-liberal narrative that denounces economic and political modernity, individualism, the destruction of so-called traditional values, and imposition of external cultural standards' (13). They also share hopes 'for a pan-European future for "white" or "Christian" peoples in which Russia would have a role' (11). According to Dugin, for the Russian people to survive as an ethnically unified group, 'it is necessary to appeal to the most radical forms of Russian nationalism' (Dugin, 2000:259). This includes 'red fascism' – 'a revolutionary, rebellious, romantic, idealistic [form of nationalism] appealing to a great myth and transcendental idea' (Dugin, 1997). Essentially anti-Western, both the Russian World concept and Dugin's neo-Eurasianism recognize state violence and military neocolonialism as primary means of mobilizing the new Russian nationalism. On 15 September 2022, several days after his daughter was assassinated, Dugin announced that Russia had entered a third world war instigated by the collective West, which he insists has been seeking the end of Russia since 1991 (Dugin, 2022). This war requires the creation of new technologies and the development of a new ideology based on the rejection of Western values, the preservation of a sovereign Russian economy, and the use of mass media, education, and culture to mobilize the population for victory.

Historically, it was the philosopher Ivan Ilyin (1883–1954) who penned a theory of Russian Christian fascism. Vladislav Surkov, the engineer of Putin's propaganda machine, subsequently transformed it into Putin's 'metaphysical and moral justification for political totalitarianism, which [Ilyin] expressed in practical outlines for a fascist state' (Snyder, 2018). A Christian thinker, Ilyin defined modernity as a 'disgrace', a world of fragments characterized by 'pluralism and its civil society' (Snyder, 2018). Fascist ideology and its matrices of leadership were central to Ilyin's redemptive model. Exiled from Soviet Russia in 1922, he was a supporter of the Russian White Movement. Later, he embraced Mussolini's regime and cooperated with the Third Reich. However, because he did not fully accept the ideological principles of Nazism and Hitler's iconic status, Ilyin left Germany for Zurich, where his focus rested with the future of Russia and its rebirth after the collapse of the Bolshevik empire. In his desire to restore the glory of the Russian empire, Putin legitimized Ilyin's ideas. According to Timothy Snyder, in 'transforming international politics into a discussion of "spiritual threats," Ilyin's works have helped Russian elites to portray Ukraine, Europe, and the United States as existential dangers to Russia' (Snyder, 2018), while the state-supported media have aided the regime in suppressing political opposition and creating a political atmosphere in which the invasion of a neighbouring country was deemed acceptable to many Russians as a holy war.

By 2022, through appropriation and mobilization of Russian grassroots nationalism, Putin's government had transformed Russian political culture into a system of governance that Lev Gudkov named a 'recurring totalitarianism' (Gudkov, 2018:255–7). Based on punitive legislations and practices that are put forward 'independently of control and responsibility to the population', recurring totalitarianism allows the state to impose norms on peoples' behaviour and prosecute actions by force (Gudkov in Senshin, 2022). For Gudkov, 'terror and repression are the outcomes of the totalitarian organization of society' (Senshin, 2022). They are based on the 'fusion of party and state . . . the cult of the leader . . ., the almightiness of the secret police, acting outside any legal frameworks . . ., the state's monopoly on mass media and its transformation into a powerful instrument of propaganda and ideological indoctrination' as well as control over civil society and the economy subjected to the political goals of the state (Gudkov in Senshin, 2022). Unlike Soviet totalitarianism, which was based on a homogeneous ideology mobilized by oppressive systems of governance – including the GULAG – and insured by the figure of the leader, Stalin, Putin's governance is based on a kind of sociopolitical contract between the state and the people. This contract presupposes favourable economic and social opportunities for the population, who in return promises not to interfere with the political operations of the state. It is secured via an elaborate system of state-controlled employment opportunities which guarantee growth in social and financial security, but it also breeds indifference to amoral behaviour in the political sphere. If domestic and foreign policies do not endanger the comfort and security of the people, the population will not impede the actions of the state and may support its activities, even an invasion of a neighbouring country. This contract effectively delegates responsibility to 'legitimize the existing social order and its constituent institutions, norms of behaviour and rituals, their origin and significance to the state' (Gudkov in Senshin, 2022). Its goal is to generate ideas and images that underpin two key performative tropes: 'the image of the enemy(s) and the utopia of restoring the archaic past' (Gudkov in Senshin, 2022). Nearly two years into the Russian-Ukrainian war, however, this recurring totalitarianism begins to look more and more like its 1930s predecessor. In its most contagious forms, Hannah Arendt reminds us, nationalism turns into a crisis of legitimacy and human dignity, or totalitarianism (Arendt, 1962:460–2). Total control of the legislature and courts, total terror, and total submission of the individual to the state are the ultimate forms of nationalism, as evidenced by Nazi Germany and Stalinist Russia. To uphold this narrative, the state uses the performative and discursive strategies of nationalist propaganda, while many of its artists produce theatre and cultural performances to resist it.

1 Performing Institutional Nationalism

Performance studies scholars have commented on how the Russian nationalist agenda is mobilized through state-funded and state-supported performances designed for international audiences – including the 2009 Eurovision Song Contest and the 2014 Winter Olympic Games – and for domestic consumption. The latter included commemorations of the victory in World War II, which involved celebrations of Victory Day and marches by the Bessmertny polk/ Immortal Regiment (Figure 1). These performative events represent the 'incarnation of the political use of history by the government elite as a tool of political argumentation' and work explicitly to assemble and mobilize the fundamental principles of nationalism (Milosevich-Juaristi, 2018). Putin's personal performances of power – his public speeches and mediatized appearances – exemplify another aspect of the performance of institutional nationalism.

Michael Billig attests that although nationalism is an elusive concept difficult to define, it often manifests as people's psychological and emotional desire to belong (Billig, 2010:43). When it comes to the construction and performance of institutional nationalism, people's emotive gestures of identification with familiar, simple, and easily identifiable figures, national symbols, and cultural practices begin to play a special role. Waving flags, using coins and banknotes that bear national emblems or images of leaders, playing national anthems in schools, and referencing canonical historical events at celebratory and commemorative ceremonies all help to mobilize patriotic ideologies and feelings, and thus constitute major dramaturgical tropes of 'banal nationalism' (37). Highly performative and 'dangerously emotional and irrational', banal nationalism is generated from the bottom up, by emotions running from fear to excitement (37). The creation of imaginary communities of people, who enter the public sphere tied by a singular objective, is the primary aim of banal

Figure 1 CIS WWII Immortal Regiment Campaign, May 5, 2023, Photo Gavriil Grigorov / POOL via AP

nationalism. It leads to the manifestation of affection, a feeling of collective belonging, which 'results from transpersonal relations between bodies and objects' and is evident in the ways these bodies and objects infect each other with patriotism (Militz & Schurr, 2016:55). 'Affective nationalism' involves the construction of a collective 'we' and conversely the conflictual and uncomfortable placement of a singular 'I' within the group. Shared history and linguistic, ethnic, religious, gendered, and territorial belonging are key elements in its making. Shared characteristics mobilize emotional and phatic powers, and the identification of a common enemy – real or constructed – cements the sense of a magic 'we' and the existence of the collective.

The annual marches of the Immortal Regiment function in this way. Originally a grassroots initiative, in 2015, the Immortal Regiment was 'co-opted by the Russian state … to promote its increasingly conservative cultural politics' using 'patriotic education and propaganda', and to provide 'mass entertainment' (Hanukai, 2020:801). These marches function as symbols of optimism, loyalty, and state power, and thus constitute good examples of institutional and banal nationalism. The Immortal Regiment project now has a specially designed website where people can share information about their dead relatives, study war heroes, and pay homage to the memory of Russian veterans. The annual marches feature ordinary Russians dressed in old uniforms, waving flags, and carrying banners and posters with photographs of dead relatives. These performative tactics are best understood as 'spectral practices that ask the living to act as surrogates for the dead' (Hanukai, 2020:803). They purposefully mobilize the affectual powers of nationalism. The posters use similar colour schemes and frame the faces of dead heroes with ribbons. They appear highly personal to the family who carries them, but also abstract and mythological.

Figure 2 is a poster produced by my own family. It depicts my maternal grandfather, who was killed at the beginning of World War II. He was a committed communist but, as a Jew, was never officially granted membership in the communist Party. In June 1941, he volunteered for the front but was killed within two weeks. He has now taken his place in the ranks of the Immortal Regiment, thanks to the efforts of his great-great-granddaughters, who are barely aware of his Jewishness or his heroism, but who participate enthusiastically in this performance of institutional nationalism. For them, a chance to participate in the marches of the Immortal Regiment and to hold the photo of their dead great-great-grandfather is a personal assertion of belonging. For me, the framed photograph plays a role in the construction of collective identity and is thus primarily a token of banal nationalism. More generally, the photographs depict thousands of Russians deeply united in a performative gesture of public assembly. Moreover, when these marches are televised, they acquire a mythological dimension. Produced both sincerely and performatively, they perfectly illustrate the state's appropriation and weaponizing of the collective trauma of the people. They gesture towards a new collective self, made manifest under Putin's gaze.

Figure 2 Lev Lazarevich Nepomnyashchy (1906–1941) Author's family archive

The figure of the strong leader is central to affective group formation. Freud's notion of 'identification' as an important factor in group formation is useful here because it manifests as our 'earliest expression of an emotional tie with another person' (Freud, 1949:60). In totalitarian systems, the figure of the leader acquires the unrestricted force of a deity, and 'members of a group stand in need of the illusion that they are equally and justly loved by their leader' (93). From Peter the Great to Joseph Stalin, Russian national doctrine has relied on the figure of the strong leader, on the personal appeal of the monarch as a conqueror of new lands and a protector of the nation. This myth was called into being to affirm 'the benefits of civilization and progress' brought about by the monarchy (Suny, 2001:35). Today, the new tsar – the protagonist and the engine of a new ideological performance – is Putin himself. He presents as the guarantor of economic prosperity and as the defender against fatal threats and disasters. His appeal to Russia's history and his identification of the collective West as the historical enemy is a mechanism for mobilizing feelings of insecurity and threat, but also a demand for the nation to unite around its leader. Yet, when Yeltsin brought Putin to power, the latter did not exhibit strong personal presence or the performance skills necessary to play the role of Father of the Nation. Instead, he reminded us of the character Danila Bagrov from the 1997 criminal drama *Brat/Brother* directed by Aleksei Balabanov (Ostrovsky, 2016:259).

After his military service in Chechnya, a charismatic young Russian returns home to a criminalized St. Petersburg. He seeks support from his older brother, who 'turns out to be a professional hitman and pulls his sibling into the city's criminal underworld' (De la Torre, 2021). This plot twist serves as a metaphor for the social strata from which Putin emerged. A native of St. Petersburg, where he also made a political career after his tenure as a KGB spy in East Germany, Putin relied heavily on his former political comrades for his Kremlin staff, while his propaganda team capitalized on his personal background as a kid from a rough neighbourhood. Like the fictional Danila, the real Putin was ready to pick up a machine gun to fight the enemies of his country. Arkady Ostrovsky picks up the tale:

> Like Danila, Putin came from 'nowhere' into this ugly and cruel world to protect his 'brothers' and effectively licensed and justified the use of extrajudicial force. Like Danila, he was a strong and positive character unconstrained by political correctness and Western convention. (Ostrovsky, 2016:260)

The political semiotics of his personal performance mythologizes Putin as rising to power to fight Russia's enemies – mostly the Chechen separatists at the time – and as resurrecting Russia's core values including 'patriotism, collectivism, *derzhavnost*' – a tradition of being a great geopolitical state power that commands the attention of other countries – and *gosudarstvennichestvo*, the primacy of the state' (Ostrovsky, 2016:264). With time, thanks partly to televised propaganda, Putin has grown into his own myth, but has also embraced a 'bricolage of imperial, Soviet, post-Soviet, post-socialist, and postmodern identities' (Schuler, 2015:137). In addition to airing Putin's official speeches, annual conversations with ordinary Russians, and New Year's Eve addresses, Russian television, which since 2000 has been largely controlled by the state, produced images that collapsed the distinction between Putin's and Russia's might. He became Russia's own and only alpha male, a 'bare-chested mountain man, virile vampire, trendy dude, custodian of endangered species, environmentalist, nightclub crooner, Formula 1 race car driver, hockey star, surrogate parent of orphaned Siberian cranes, and more recently, fisherman extraordinaire' (137). With Russia's invasion of Ukraine in 2022, Putin's personal theatrics changed again: the militaristic rhetoric intensified, and his appearances became more focused and solemn. His televised address to the Federal Assembly on 30 September 2022, when he announced a reunification of four Ukrainian territories – the Donetsk and Lugansk republics, Zaporizhzhia, and the Kherson regions – with Russia, and the meeting-concert *Vybor ludey: Vmeste navsegda!/ Peoples' Choice: Together Forever!*, which took place in Moscow's Red Square on the same September afternoon, exemplify both Putin's personal performance of power and the tropes of institutional nationalism. They are both worth considering in more detail.

Although neither Ukraine nor the West recognized the September 2022 reunification as legitimate, Putin's televised address justified Russia's position, using rhetorical tropes and discursive images he had been rehashing since his 2007 appearance at the Munich Security Conference, a historical watershed in Russia's relations with the West. The annexation of the four Ukrainian territories was a milestone in Putin's campaign against the West and a next step in his mobilization of the Russian World concept. Putin opened his address by acknowledging the right of Donbass' people to express their territorial sovereignty, citing the UN Declaration of Human Rights. He recounted the historical unity of Russia and Ukraine, for which he insisted 'our ancestors fought', and placed the new war on par with Russia's imperial achievements. Not the most charismatic of public speakers, he nevertheless used his rhetoric and intonations to legitimize the falsified results of the referendums his administration had staged in Donbass. In conjunction with nuclear threats against Ukraine, NATO, and the collective West, he used the illocutionary power of his public speech to transform his words into actions. Calling Russians to unite against their enemies, Putin cited his favourite philosopher, Ivan Ilyin, and so framed the 2022 annexation of Ukrainian territories as one more step in repairing the damage caused by the collapse of the USSR. Yet Putin's major addressee was not the people of Ukraine, but the collective West, specifically US President Joe Biden, who has taken a firm lead in supporting the Ukrainian war effort.

More than 180,000 people attended the *Peoples' Choice* meeting/concert, which was also streamed across Russia. With excessive theatricality and emotional appeal, it was intended to dispel the atmosphere of fear, anxiety, and collective doom that marked the reception of Putin's speech, and to mobilize feelings of patriotism, loyalty, and faith in a Russian victory. In this regard, the location of the concert – Red Square with the audience facing St. Basil's Cathedral – held special significance. Built on the orders of Ivan the Terrible between 1555 and 1561, the cathedral commemorates the fall of Kazan and Astrakhan to Russia. For centuries, it served as one of Russia's major cultural symbols, both as the site of the country's official celebrations but also of protest. In January 2012, the famous feminist punk group Pussy Riot performed their number 'Putin Zassal/Putin Has Pissed Himself' on Lobnoe Mesto, a thirteen-metre-long stone platform in front of the cathedral.

Among the TV personalities, war heroes, officials, singers, and theatre artists who addressed the crowds at *Peoples' Choice*, the appearance of Ivan Okhlobystin, a theatre actor turned priest and internet influencer, deserves special mention. In a highly theatrical speech, Okhlobystin called for the renaming of Russia's special operation in Ukraine as a holy war, and in so doing upstaged Putin. His calls for a renewal of Russian patriotism escalated the emotional force of the meeting-concert to levels of massive hysteria and expressions of loyalty and supplication reminiscent of Hitler's Germany. He effectively relegitimized Putin's war and nationalist project as sacred.

In the second part of the meeting/concert, officials from Donbass and Kherson made appearances, as did Putin himself. A group of artists from Kherson, Melitopol, Lugansk, and the Republic of Bashkortostan, accompanied by the Academic Song and Dance Ensemble of the National Guard of the Russian Federation (conducted by Viktor Eliseev), sang Bulat Okudzhava's 1969 song 'Nam nuzhna odna pobeda/We Need One Victory'. Written by a poet who experienced World War II first-hand, the song commemorates the fallen. Emotional and melancholic, it serves as a warning against ambitious dreams of military victories, which never come without a human cost. For years, the song functioned as one of the most remarkable anti-war anthems in Soviet Russia, but it has been reappropriated by the propaganda machine in Putin's time. Performed in the context of the Ukrainian war, the song signified, even if only performatively and just on the concert's stage, the Russian World in action. Presented under the banner 'Together Forever', the song ended with the performers shouting patriotic slogans, such as 'we are Russia, Donbass is Russia, Russia is us!' In this instance, the festivities in Red Square were intended to instil feelings of happiness, enthusiasm, and communality: all characteristic of affective nationalism. To intensify this effect, the dramaturgy of the event relied on visual symbols of Russian nationalism, including the collective waving of Russian tricolours on and off stage. The national flag was used to symbolize 'the sacred character of the nation' because it was 'revered by loyal citizens and ritually defiled by those who wish to make a protest' (Billig, 2010:41).

Furthermore, carefully cast headliners who had openly sworn their loyalty to the state gave weight to this performance of allegiance and nationalism. They included a blue-eyed singer, Shaman, with expensive-looking blond dread-locks; an old-timer, Oleg Gazmanov, the author of the 2005 nationalist song 'Sdelan v SSSR/Made in the USSR'; and a famous actor, Vladimir Mashkov, who for years has been an open supporter of Putin's regime.

In 2014, Mashkov espoused Russia's illegal annexation of Crimea and Sevastopol. In 2018, he endorsed Putin's bid for re-election and served as his representative. Also in 2018, Mashkov became the artistic director of the Oleg Tabakov (Tabakerka) Theatre, the first theatre company in Moscow to put a 'Z' banner on its façade in 2022. In 2022, he backed Russia's full-scale invasion of Ukraine and performed during its propaganda rally, which took place on 18 March 2022 at Luzhniki Stadium. On 4 December 2023, at the Extraordinary IX (XXIII) Congress of the Russian Union of Theatre Workers (STD), Mashkov was elected as the new chairman of the Russian Union of Theatre Workers. Several days after the election, Mashkov joined Putin's 2024 presidential campaign headquarters, as one of its co-chairs.

The significance of the 'Z' symbol in Russia's military campaign against Ukraine cannot be underestimated. Not only it is used by the propaganda machine, Russian army, and ordinary people to signal their support of the war, it has been equated with the Nazi swastika and subsequently banned from public use in many Western countries. There are several explanations for the Latin letters 'Z' and 'V' becoming symbols of Russia's aggression in Ukraine. For some pro-Putin military experts, 'the letter "Z" stood for the last name of the Ukrainian President, Zelensky, and "V" and "O" for his first name and patronymic, Volodymyr Oleksandrovych' (Gessen, 2022). For Russia's Ministry of Defence, the letter 'Z' stands for 'the first letter of the Russian word "za" ("for"), so "Z" could mean "for victory", "for peace", "for truth", and "for the children of Donbass"' (Gessen, 2022). 'Graphically, the "Z" is clearly closer to the swastika than to any prominent Soviet symbol, such as the five-pointed star, the hammer and sickle, or the red flag', and its use is directly linked to Russia's victory over Nazi Germany and by extension to Putin's justifications for the war in Ukraine, such as his responsibility to fight the Nazis in the Ukrainian leadership (Gessen, 2022). This reasoning 'require[s] a double inversion: first, the people of Ukraine – a nation that suffered some of the greatest losses at the hands of Nazi Germany and one that is currently led by a Jewish President – are rendered as Nazis; then, the Russians, who claim to be fighting for peace and "de-Nazification", adopt a visual symbol that appears to reference the swastika' (Gessen, 2022). Displaying a 'Z' symbol on the façade of a state-owned building, someone's private window, or a vehicle is highly performative: it signifies the owner's support of the government's policies, which, in Mashkov's case, also enhances his personal patriotic stance. After authorizing the appearance of the 'Z' symbol on the façade of the Tabakerka Theatre on 29 March 2022, he felt 'proud that his institution has put on "this symbol for the motherland, for our army, for our president"' (Mashkov in Sitdikov, 2022).

On 21 July 2022, the EU Council Implementing Regulation (EU) No 269/2014 imposed sanctions on Mashkov because he 'actively supported Russia's war of aggression against Ukraine' and so is considered 'responsible for actively supporting or implementing actions or policies which undermine or threaten the territorial integrity, sovereignty and independence of Ukraine, or stability or security in Ukraine' (Council Implementing Regulation (EU) 2022/1270).

Gender plays another important role in the performances of nationalism. On the stage of *Peoples' Choice*, the headliners stood for an image of whiteness and toxic masculinity and conveyed feelings of stability, continuity, and a secure future. Together, these figures reinforced the state's nationalist and colonialist agenda, its aspirations for the dominance of the Russian World. Cast in the roles of mothers, devoted wives, and daughters of war heroes, female participants were called on to exhibit maximum support to their male counterparts and so to reinforce patriarchy as one of the foundations of the Russian state. Some of them, including a young doctor wounded in her legs and the wife of a newly drafted soldier, were presented as heroines in their own right. The appearance of Bogdana Neshcheret, a sixteen-year-old poet and private in the Ghost Brigade from the Donbass, who was awarded the Medal for Valour and Courage, crowned this performance. After Bogdana recited her poem to Russia, the concert anchor announced her secret dream – to meet President Putin in person – was to finally come true. As if by magic, Putin appeared on stage in a performative gesture as the Father of the Nation. After the concert ended, Bogdana presented Putin with her poetry while the president invited Bogdana to publish her work as a book (Figure 3).

Figure 3 Vladimir Putin and Bogdana Neshcheret,
Russia_New_Territories_Accession_Celebrations. Sept. 30, 2022.
Photo Michail Doudin / Sputnik via AP

Figure 4 Stalin and Gelya (Engelsina) Markizova, 1936.

A number of commentators have already suggested an affinity between Stalin's cult of personality and Putin's. The latter's encounter with Bogdana reinforced this connection by evoking the iconography of Soviet children thanking their collective father, Stalin, for their happy childhood. In 1936, the *Pravda* newspaper published a photograph 'Friend of the Little Children', which depicted Stalin with a little girl in his arms (Figure 4). The girl was Engelsina (Gelya) Markizova (1928–2004) from The Buryat Autonomous Soviet Socialist Republic, whose father, Ardan, was later accused of being a Japanese spy and shot in 1938, and whose mother, Dominika, was exiled to Kazakhstan and died in 1938 (Egorov, 2018).

The child soldier Bogdana played a similar role in Putin's performance of power in 2022. Publicly granting her wish served Putin's dramaturgs not only by acting as a symbolic bridge back to Stalin, but also by bolstering their own myth-making. Any girl – be she a fighter, heroine, or poet – is primarily figured as a damsel in distress awaiting protection from a strong male figure, in this case the Father of the Nation, Putin himself. To consolidate the impression, the encounter with Bogdana was followed by Putin's speech anticipating victory and his participation in performing Russia's national anthem by lip-syncing into the muted microphone.

Scholars of nationalism have commented widely on the symbolic power of national anthems, their 'patriotic language', and the ways they 'invoke emotions and ties to a nation' (Hummel, 2017:227). For Putin, the Russian national anthem has special value. One of his 'first symbolic steps as president was to restore the Soviet national anthem, originally composed in 1938 – at the height of Stalin's great terror – as a hymn to the Bolshevik party' (Ostrovsky, 2016:268). Yeltsin had replaced the Soviet anthem with Mikhail Glinka's 'Patriotic Song', but Putin decided to 'bring back the old tune, albeit with new lyrics, which were promptly supplied by the author of the two previous Soviet versions', Sergey Mikhalkov (268). In this way, the connection between the glorious Soviet past and Putin's new present was to be restored and Putin's place on the throne of the new empire legitimized.

2 An *Enfant Terrible* of Russian Nationalism

This section is the first in a series of case studies that examine plays, practitioners, and theatre projects that challenge the homogenizing narratives of nationalism in Russia. In so doing they expose the contentious binary of individual versus state, and criticize state violence and police brutality as behavioural norms. Kirill Serebrennikov is one example of a practitioner who has paid a high price for engaging in such work, and this section explores his key achievements.

A recipient of numerous theatre awards in Russia and abroad, Serebrennikov was one of the most flamboyant artists to emerge in Russia during Putin's rule. Yet, due to accusations of financial fraud, house arrest (August 2017–April 2019), and a public trial (June 2020) that kept Russian and international theatre communities on the edge of their seats, Serebrennikov has become persona non grata in the Russian theatre scene. Between 2011 and 2014, he ran the Moscow centre of contemporary arts Platforma as a part of President Medvedev's culture program of modernization. Anastasia Boutsko explains: '[A] magnet for young, innovative theatre practitioners, over six years *Platforma* staged more than 340 theatre projects ranging from chamber plays for small audiences to events in packed stadiums . . . Serebrennikov's personal style of directing was characterised by a fusion of theatre, film, modern dance, new media, and music' (Boutsko, 2020).

After Putin returned to power in 2012, the modernization project was scrapped. Traditional ideologies and conservative values were to be retained, both at the level of artistic practice and also through new legislations, which privileged 'the most archaic needs emanating from the very depths of the national psyche, namely the imperial idea which, paradoxically, unites Russian Orthodox traditions with the glorification of the Soviet past' (Davydova, 2018). The conservative historian Vladimir Medinsky was appointed the minister of culture. Platforma subsequently attracted the unwelcome attention of the authorities, with Medinsky, the Russian Orthodox Church, and the FSB combining forces against Serebrennikov and his company. In June 2020, they were charged with embezzling state funds, so the trial – renamed a 'theatre trial' by Serebrennikov's supporters – has turned into a lesson in political and personal obedience taught by the Russian authorities. It reminded Russia's artistic community that, in this country, the state and theatre are always tightly interconnected. After the trial ended with a substantial fine for Serebrennikov, he continued to run his Gogol Centre, where he had been appointed artistic director in 2012. In February 2021, his contract was not renewed. After his fine was paid, thanks to the patronage of the oligarch Boris Abramovich, Serebrennikov left Russia, while the Gogol Centre was closed by the authorities in June 2022. In spring 2022, Serebrennikov expressed his anti-war position on the conflict in Ukraine and joined the many Russian artists who left the country in a gesture of protest. Today, Serebrennikov resides in Germany and works on theatre and film projects across Europe.

Although it is difficult to ascertain the precise reasons the Russian state decided to make Serebrennikov the object of its performance of power, to a certain degree, I argue in this section, the director fell victim to his own artistic project of resistance to nationalism. Provocation – artistic, political, personal – is Serebrennikov's signature style. Adapting Russian canonical literature, advocating for new theatre writing, transposing films to stage, and modernizing opera and ballet are signature features of his directorial approach. Asking difficult ethical questions about personal conformism and responsibility, interrogating the historical and political narratives of Russian officialdom, and condemning state violence constitute thematic through lines in his work, which often turns aesthetics into politics. Cosmopolitanism is Serebrennikov's world view, and it was exemplified in his multilingual and multicultural company. The Gogol Centre was a rare example of a Russian state theatre hiring non-ethnically Russian actors. Postmodern theatricality and post-dramatic grotesque also mark Serebrennikov's theatrical vocabulary, although in its educational objectives his theatre recalls Bertolt Brecht's political project in which estrangement served as a mechanism of distancing, but also as a tool of resistance. Outsiders – a teenage social outcast, a political dissident, an intellectual, and even a police officer who accidentally falls out of the system – are the protagonists of Serebrennikov's theatre. Positioned at some distance from the norms of social behaviour dictated by the state, these characters allow Serebrennikov to reveal, examine, and condemn the mechanisms of Putin's panopticon, which is enforced by such oppressive systems of social control as family, school, and police precinct.

Born in 1969 in the city of Rostov-on-Don, Serebrennikov grew up on the cultural fringes of the Soviet empire, and his personal and professional coming of age was marked by a sense of internal exile and a desire for freedom. Rejected by a Moscow theatre school at the age of seventeen, he returned home, where he pursued a degree in physics at Rostov University while directing numerous theatre productions, working for the local TV station, and winning his first awards. Serebrennikov came back to Moscow to direct Vassiliy Sigarev's *Plasticine* (2002) at the Centre of Dramaturgy and Directing. This was his personal breakthrough as a director and the beginning of an illustrious career for himself and for the actors involved. An outsider in Moscow's theatre establishment, Serebrennikov felt free from local politics and tastes, and this determined his choices in dramatic repertoire and directorial style. Moreover, his work tackled 'social issues, something that is scorned by traditional Russian theatre, where art is supposed to deal with the eternal, not the ephemeral' (Davydova, 2018). Sigarev's *Plasticine* was one such play.

A recipient of the 2001 Anti-Booker Prize, it was an experiment in hyperrealism, non-normative language, and theatrical violence. It belonged to the New Drama movement that began flourishing on the Russian stage in the mid-1990s. These plays focused on the troublesome realities of Boris Yeltzin's time and introduced new forms in dramatic writing, which demanded reforms in directing. Claiming its origins in documentary theatre, *Plasticine* told the tragic story of a small-town boy, Maxim, who at the age of fourteen is bullied by his peers and his teachers. Surrounded by violence, Maxim must turn into an aggressor in order to survive. Because of its status as a 'metaphor for cynical violence' in 'the post-Soviet civil war', the play did not appeal to Moscow's more established directors, although it did chime with Serebrennikov's own experiences growing up (Beumers & Lipovetsky, 2009:153). By staging *Plasticine*, he diagnosed the identity crisis that characterized the post-Soviet era and instigated a powerful project of artistic provocation based on the notion of uncomfortable truth. He also recognized the symbolic potential of a play driven by social doom, and so opted for 'the form of an antique tragedy' to express the trauma of his generation (Serebrennikov, 2009:11).

The production was somewhat eclectic. 'The actors all played a variety of different roles', while 'a chorus of old women dressed in black' accompanied the action (Beumers & Lipovetsky, 2009:159). Politically, *Plasticine* critiqued Yeltzin's Russia, but it did not seek to openly confront or challenge the regime; instead it asked questions about one's social, moral, and ethical responsibilities. It addressed younger spectators who were feverishly seeking clarity about their place in their communities and in the wider world. Because it asked unnerving questions about personal conformity, the production not only altered Moscow's theatrical landscape, it also 'sculpted the fate of an entire generation of artists' (Rajkina, 2002). Sererbennikov's work became a 'favourite of the liberal intelligentsia', even as it irritated 'cultural conservatives', who considered 'his frequent use of onstage nudity and obscene language, as well as modern adaptations of classics, a step too far' (Nikerichev, 2020).

Serebrennikov's 2004 production of *Playing the Victim* by the Presnyakov brothers for the Moscow Art Theatre became his next important intervention in the investigation of family and state violence.[2] A kind of spoof on Shakespeare's *Hamlet*, *Playing the Victim* tells a story of a young man, Valya, whose name denotes his androgynous identity and whose job is to play the victims of murder – mostly women – during forensic crime scene reconstructions. Unlike in Plasticine, however, Valya is placed inside the police system, so brutality and systemic violence

[2] In 2006, Sererbennikov directed a film, *Playing the Victim*, the analysis of which is beyond the scope of this Element.

emerge as the norm, as reflected in the farcical-philosophical style of Presnyakovs' dramaturgy. As the play opens, the ghost of Valya's father, who has been poisoned by his mother and uncle, pays him a visit, seeking revenge for his murder. Unable to differentiate between reality and role play, 'Valia takes on the role of the criminal himself: he poisons mother, uncle and girlfriend, arranging the bodies accurately in the silhouettes drawn on the floor' (Beumers & Lipovetsky 2009:292).

Neglected by his family, abused by his superiors at the police precinct, and victimized by general disrespect for a human life as perpetuated by the Russian state, Valya's fate on the stage of Serebrennikov's production illustrates the off-stage violence of Putin's 'postmodern fascism', which can turn anyone – 'a class enemy, a sexual opponent, the neighbour, the colleague, the relative and even a child' – into a proverbial Other and a scapegoat to the state machine (Beumers & Lipovetsky, 2009:282). This otherness is 'arbitrary and floating', so Serebrennikov staged the everyday violence as something playful and highly theatrical. He turned reality into the grotesque, in which playing the victim and playing the killer go hand in hand (282). In Putin's Russia, the production suggested, it is 'only through violence' that people 'gain a sense of belonging to the "large national body"' (284). By extension, in a country that embraces systemic violence and, as Serebrennikov argued in his production, in a society that lacks basic compassion, calls for a holy war in Ukraine came as unsurprising, even if not fully expected.

It is not by chance that Serebrennikov chose Martin McDonagh's *The Pillowman* (2003) for his next production. Its action unfolds in a fictional totalitarian state somewhere in Eastern Europe, where two police detectives are interrogating an influential writer, Katurian Katurian, whose fictional murder stories bear a suspicious resemblance to a series of real crimes. The detectives assume the writer is also the killer. Serebrennikov transposed McDonagh's setting to a clearly recognizable contemporary Moscow, where state violence and police brutality had been internalized and embraced by ordinary people. In terms of staging, Serebrennikov again opted for hyperrealism and heighted theatricality, choreographing scenes of physical violence. His detectives were 'complex-stricken apparatchiks who treat their victim with hatred and respect' (Davydova, 2007). A reviewer described one detective as 'a homosexual sadistic perverted Komsomol member' and another as 'chopped-up, axe-wielding party scum' (Davydova, 2007). The trio 'played out witty circus numbers', with a scene involving a horrific beating transformed 'into a virtuoso dance' (Shenderova, 2007). The major question Serebrennikov asked was about the moral responsibility of the artist for crimes committed by their country, which created clear links between the fictional world of McDonagh's play and Putin's Russia. By agreeing on the social contract proposed by their government, Serebrennikov further suggested, Russian people were easily becoming both accomplices and victims of the state's crimes.

Otmorozki/ Scumbags (2011), based on Zakhar Prilepin's novel *San'ka*, was Serebrennikov's next major attempt to explore the complex interdependency between the individual and the state. Created for Platforma, *Scumbags* opened in Berlin at the 2011 Festival of International New Drama (FIND). It depicted a group of radical twenty-year-old political rebels pitted against riot police of the same age. Casting students from his acting class at the Moscow Art Theatre Studio, Serebrennikov instructed the young performers to go onto the streets, participate in protests, talk to activists, and use their new knowledge to improve the script (Sila Kul'tury, 2017). This was a new method of seeking theatrical truth for the director. The truth of real-life experience was to be added to his theatre vocabulary of political protest.

In 2013, now an artistic director of the Gogol Centre, Serebrennikov staged *Idioty/The Idiots*, which was based on Lars Von Trier's eponymous film. He was spellbound by Trier's political dystopia and recast the Danish director's social dropouts as political protesters in Moscow, making references to both Russian political activists and mediatized political trials that were recognizable to his audience. For Serebrennikov, the artistic language of Dogma 95, pioneered by Lars Von Trier and Thomas Vinterberg on screen, was another approach to putting truth on a theatre stage and thus one of the major devices in his production. He authored his own Theatre Dogma 13 manifesto in which he called on others to 'reject imitation of action, lighting effects and external sounds' on stage (Sila Kul'tury, 2017).

In adopting these artistic tactics, Serebrennikov remained a devotee of the New Drama movement and its political project expressed through documentary and testimonial theatre as practised by Moscow's Teatr.doc. Yet, if the politics of the Gogol Centre referenced the New Drama movement and Teatr.doc, in its aesthetics, Serebrennikov's theatre offered a radical contrast to the entire tradition of Russian documentary theatre. His Gogol Centre brought real people, objects, and histories on stage, but the style of its productions was 'glamour incarnate, with its spiffy designs, international projects, and trendsetting ambitions' (Freedman, 2020:89). The company enjoyed a sold-out box office despite high ticket prices and also managed to make a lasting political impact. As John Freedman notes, like Teatr.doc, 'which often hosted hot-topic evenings highlighting important political people or events, the Gogol Centre regularly scheduled lectures, meetings, and film screenings that touched on controversial issues' and thus aimed to nurture its audience's political consciousness, inner freedom, and dignity (89). Serebrennikov's 2016 performance/installation *Pokhorony Stalina/Stalin's Funeral*, written by Mikhail Kaluzhsky, was among its most powerful productions. Its objectives were to bury Stalin for good, to remember the victims of his regime, and to question the legitimacy of his myth.

Stalin's Funeral exemplifies a type of performance activism that uses re-enactment to mourn the past and forewarn about the future. It aims explicitly to activate the audiences' historical and political consciousness, and thus has the potential to be disruptive. Serebrennikov invited Kaluzhsky, a political journalist and playwright whose work revolves around questions of truth and reconciliation, to write a documentary script in which the events and atmosphere of the great funeral were to be re-enacted. The day of Stalin's state funeral, 9 March 1953, was marked by tragedy when hundreds of people, who had come to pay their last respects to the dictator, were crushed to death in the crowd. To create a dramatic counterpoint to these events, Kaluzhsky brought another death and another funeral into play.

By coincidence, the Russian composer Sergei Prokofiev had died at home in Moscow on the same day as Stalin, 5 March 1953. Prokofiev's funeral was a morbid farce, and only a small number of people were able to pay their respects and attend the ceremony. To reinforce this sense of historical injustice, Kaluzhsky augmented archival documents, personal testimonies, and literary artefacts relating to Stalin's funeral, with a narrative detailing the milestones of Prokofiev's life.

Prokofiev had made an irreversible error of judgement when he returned to the USSR in 1936 after years of political exile. By offering his services to Stalin, the famous composer effectively made himself a tragic character in his own story. In 1948, he was attacked for his anti-democratic formalism. In its reflective dramaturgy of historical juxtapositions, *Stalin's Funeral* explored the rise and fall of an artist whose life and death can be recognized as a counter-narrative to the myth of the great dictator. Moreover, by focusing this counter-narrative on an individual, Kaluzhsky evoked the Foucauldian postulate of monumental history, the history of the state, devouring the stories and the lives of its citizens.

In its performative composition, *Stalin's Funeral* further reinforced this juxtaposition between the state and its people and tried to give agency to neglected voices of history. It aimed to stage the untreated injuries of the past and the omnipresent fear that characterized both the public and private lives of Soviet citizens. Staged as a kind of performance/ceremony, it offered a theatrical visualization of history underscored by eyewitnesses' accounts of the funeral and by historical research and personal reflections narrated by contemporary writers, artists, journalists, and human rights activists.

Among these accounts, the testimony of the theatre scholar Aleksey Bartoshevich, who witnessed the funeral first-hand, deserves special mention. The Bartoshevich family lived near where Stalin's coffin was displayed. While out for a stroll, young Aleksey suddenly saw a crowd approach. He froze on the spot, unable to comprehend the hypnotic magnitude of the bodies marching toward their idol. This crowd – he remembers – was mostly made up of middle-aged men, already traumatized by their experiences in the Great Patriotic War. As the crowd moved toward its destination, it became more and more violent: suddenly – he recalls – powerful cries of 'for Motherland', 'for Stalin', could be heard, something Soviet soldiers used on the battlefield. The movement of the mourners and their chanting turned the procession into a spectacle of mythological proportions. As the crowd surged by, the boy escaped its deadly power by hiding in a nearby building.

To evoke similar feelings of danger and excitement on stage, Serebrennikov used a chorus of live performers. Positioned in tight rows across the stage, the constricted configuration of bodies created the effect of a crowd with people jostling and crashing into each other. Dressed in contemporary clothing, the performers moved together, back and forth, up and down, without actually leaving their designated spots. Squeezed against each other, they formed a faceless entity, a highly symbolic image of the unidentified victims not only of the day of Stalin's funeral, but also of the excesses of his regime. To reinforce a sense of suffocation, Serebrennikov juxtaposed the movement of the crowd with the projection of documentary footage of the actual historical event, in which ancestors of the young artists and spectators were losing their lives while worshipping their idol. The joining together of documentary footage, oral testimonies of eyewitnesses, performative re-enactment of the energy of the crowd, and scenes from Prokofiev's life generated powerful political effects (Figures 5 and 6). By bringing documents and testimonies into the theatrical space, *Stalin's Funeral* constructed a new living archive, challenging the energy of the past through the work of its performers and spotlighting the relationship between the past and the politics of its mythologizing in the present. Contextualization was a recurring trope.

The performance began with spectators entering the lobby of the Gogol Centre and finding an installation organized by the Moscow's GULAG

Figure 5 *Stalin's Funeral*, directed by Kirill Serebrennikov, Gogol Centre, 2016, Photo by Ira Polyarnaya

Figure 6 *Stalin's Funeral*, directed by Kirill Serebrennikov, Gogol Centre, 2016, Photo by Ira Polyarnaya

History Museum greeting them. This involved 'photo stands of those who died in the GULAG or were repressed but survived' with each stand 'embedded into the floor with a piece of cement' (Emel'yanenko, 2016). The photographs, Serebrennikov explains, 'portray people of various professions: academics, translators, workers, professors of the Moscow Conservatory. When you look at these faces, you realize that the best people of Russia have been killed' (RIA NOVOSTI, 2016).

As spectators moved into the auditorium, they encountered another installation: 'The stage awaited the audience with mountains of galoshes, mittens, coats, and handfuls of coat buttons' (Emel'yanenko, 2016). This image evoked another familiar trope of history. Often, piles of shoes, suitcases, spectacles, and abandoned objects stand for the victims of the Holocaust and as a reminder of the atrocities committed by the Nazis. Likewise, *Stalin Funeral* aimed to commemorate the victims of Stalin's regime and to accuse the perpetrators. It also worked to resist the fossilization of memory. By exposing the mechanisms of myth-making, it served as an event of counter-commemoration and disruption, and by extension as a device for resisting nationalism.

In 2021, Serebrennikov returned to the period of Stalinist purges in his production of Dmitri Shostakovich's opera *The Nose* (1928) for the Bavarian State Opera. He directed most of the show via Zoom while still in Russia paying off his fine. For Serebrennikov, Shostakovich's opera, which was based on Nikolay Gogol's 1836 short story of the same name, anticipated the 'terror and fear [that] changed the whole of Russian society' (Behrens, 2021). Staging it in 2021, the director wanted to reveal similarities between the late 1920s and the political climate of contemporary Russia. Serebrennikov transposed Shostakovich's setting into the gloomy and grotesque St. Petersburg of the early 2020s, with the police precinct the place of safety for the opera's protagonist, Sergeant Kovalev (Figures 7 and 8).

Typically a location from which to exercise power over ordinary people who are prisoners of the system, the precinct turns into the place of Kovalev's nightmares when he wakes up one morning to discover his nose – his identity – is gone. This is the existential tragedy of a small man who lives within a totalitarian system. When he loses his nose, Kovalev is ostracized and ejected from the system and thus joins the list of Serebrennikov's outsiders – the protagonists of the margins. Yet Kovalev has no clear moral standing. He is a kind of small screw in the system whose tragedy is the focus of Hannah Arendt's political writing and her concept of the banality of evil. This is Russia as an enormous police precinct in which 'the only way out of this stage-prison is to go to prison' (Surzha, 2021).

Figure 7 *Die Nase* by Dmitri Shostakovich, directed by Kirill Serebrennikov. The Bavarian State Opera, 2021. Photographer Wilfried Hösl.

Figure 8 *Die Nase* by Dmitri Shostakovich, directed by Kirill Serebrennikov. The Bavarian State Opera, 2021. Photographer Wilfried Hösl.

However, when Kovalev is ejected from the system, he learns no lessons and does not change. Seeking to draw attention to his loss, he turns to the media. In the world of the production, everything is performative: news is fake, protests are choreographed, and support rallies – very much like Putin's meeting-concert – are staged and televised. Kovalev does not understand that in this context, he can be cancelled twice: first, when his nose leaves him and he no longer fits this world; and second, when he loses access to the state-sponsored media and his mediatized reflection. Being forced to observe the world from the outside does not make Kovalev ask himself a single question about the corrupt system, however. His only goal is to retrieve his nose so that he can go back to being part of the system.

Meanwhile, the production goes berserk. A scene of New Year's celebrations with a chorus of riot police dressed as Russian grannies with balalaikas melts into a political protest with people carrying NET and NEIN posters and getting piled into a cardboard police truck. Documentary footage of real protests is projected as the action evolves into an absurd spectacle. A celebrity figure is brought on stage in her own coffin to sign photos and to prepare the staging of her own funeral, while a group of government supporters fills the stage, shouting DA and waving flags bearing the image of a clean-shaven leader, perhaps Putin himself.

Unable to regain his position, Kovalev starts to lose his mind, a defence mechanism because his madness allows an escape from a world of pain into one of fantasy. The iconic symbols of St. Petersburg, police trucks, and snowblowers turn into cardboard flats and theatrical props, which signify both the performative world of Russian state power and Kovalev's warped imagination. The culmination of Shostakovich's phantasmagoria is a huge nose emerging on stage with devils jumping around it.

Elsewhere characters wear grotesque masks covered with oversized noses. When Kovalev loses his nose, his humanity begins to emerge. But he is embarrassed and ashamed by his difference in world of conformity. When his nose returns, Kovalev immediately reverts to his former self. His 'pathological hatred of people comes to the surface once again' and the 'recently humiliated perpetrator, Kovalev begins to gleefully beat up the prisoners of his precinct' (Surzha, 2021). In Serebrennikov's hands, Shostakovich's opera turns into a political statement about contemporary Russia, where only by being an outsider can one remain a decent person. According to Arseniy Surzha, Serebrennikov's Russia 'is a police state. In Shakespeare's drama the world is a theatre, in Serebrennikov's theatre, the world is a police station . . . No matter who you might be, if you live in a state driven by police ideology, you turn into its by-product' (Surzha, 2021).

In July 2022, Serebrennikov's staging of Chekhov's 1893 short story *The Чёрный Mönch/The Black Monk* opened at the Avignon Festival, while the Moscow Department of Culture closed his Gogol Centre for good. This closure brought an end to the creative and political freedoms that Serebrennikov's work had come to signify in Putin's Russia. Under such a regime, an artist like Serebrennikov can be only in prison, in exile, or in the wings.

3 Myth-Making and Myth-Breaking of Nationalism

In Russia, history is particularly unstable. From Peter the Great to Stalin, each new political regime engaged in a re-conceptualizing and rewriting of the country's past in order to support its new nation-building project and bolster propaganda. When the Soviet Union collapsed, each of its former republics, including the Russian Federation, faced an identity crisis. From Ukraine to Georgia, from Latvia to Kazakhstan, each newly formed post-Soviet state embarked on a journey of self-reflection. Russia, which was the economic, political, and cultural centre of the Soviet empire, failed in this task, and so turned to history to ground its sense of national identity. The ideologues of Putin's regime opted for the reappropriation of key moments in Soviet history, specifically its World War II narratives, to shape new connections between the country's past and present via narratives of sacrifice and suffering.

This is a well-known trope of ethnonationalism (Smith, 2001:63–4). Based on connecting people (*ethnos*) to their land by commemorating historical events – especially those 'misfortunes and exploits' that affected the community – ethnonationalism celebrates heroes and worships the graves of glorious ancestors, who 'bear witness to the uniqueness and antiquity of the nation' (Koulos, 2021:485). Historical narratives, monuments, personalities, and sites are co-opted by the state. As Thanos Koulos notes, by 'recalling dramatic events, symbolic crises or turning points in the history of the community and by endowing them with foci of creative energy', ethnonationalist strategies work to present the community and its territory as 'an ancestral homeland' (486). Under Putin, Russia's history became a special target for ideological control by the authorities, and the project of reinterpretation of the past was brought to life by new legislation as well as propaganda techniques.

In this context, restoring forgotten, lost, or silenced historical figures and documents constitutes an act of resistance to ethnonationalism. Russian documentary theatre, specifically its leading company Teatr.doc, exemplifies this practice. It brings the experiences of ordinary people on stage to create counter-narratives which problematize the glorified versions offered by the state. By working with the document as a source of historical memory, 'documentary theatre actualises issues of trauma, reconciliation, and forgiveness, fiction and truth' while also making visible crises in 'rejection, exile, ideology and history, borders, citizenship, and human rights' (Kaluzhsky 2015). It turns historical memory into a political statement and problematizes the tropes of ethnonationalism.

The documentary theatre of Anastasia Patlay and Nana Grinstein illustrates this practice. It brings the contemporary and historical stories of marginalized people, including political prisoners, women, migrants, and members of the LGTBQ+ community, into the theatrical spotlight. Juxtaposing personal histories with the monumental narratives of the state constitutes a core strategy in their political activism. By helping audiences recognize and denounce resentment of marginalized people as an ideological and affective trope of ethnonationalism, Patlay and Grinstein condemn Putin's regime and also offer an alternative image of Russian society in which the experience of the marginalized is recentred.

Using Olga Malinova's work on symbolic politics (Malinova, 2018), this section examines Patlay and Grinstein's project *Memoria*, which opened on the brink of Russia's invasion of Ukraine (February 2022) and became the artists' last work to be presented in Russia before their exile. By exposing and interweaving three historical layers of state oppression, *Memoria* reveals and critiques the false and damaging premises of nationalism.

When Yeltzin came to power, he began rebuilding Russia's national identity by refocusing its historical narratives. In 1995, the Russian parliament passed a law, 'On the Perpetuation of the Victory of the Soviet People in the Great Patriotic War of 1941–1945', intended to help the state regulate interpretations of the Soviet past, specifically World War II (The State Duma, 1995). During Putin's presidency, this law has undergone many amendments – in 2009, 2014, 2019, and twice in 2021 – most of which were of a prohibiting and censoring nature.

In 2014, legislation called 'On Amendments to Certain Legislative Acts of the Russian Federation', widely known as 'the law about historical memory' and against 'the rehabilitation of Nazism', prohibited dissemination of any information discrediting, challenging, or disrespecting military glory associated with the defence of the Fatherland (The State Duma, 2014). A 2019 amendment targeted production of so-called unpatriotic content. It was further supported by the 2021 law called 'On Amendments to the Federal Law on Perpetuating the Victory of the Soviet People in the Great Patriotic War of 1941–1945', which prohibits 'denying the decisive role of the Soviet people in the defeat of Nazi Germany and the humanitarian mission of the USSR in the liberation of Europe' (The State Duma, 2021).

Violations of these laws were to be punished by substantial fines, forced labor, or imprisonment. In this way, the state reinstated its monopoly on historical memory, reversing the processes of privatization for which *perestroika* had laid a foundation. This overbearing desire of the Russian government to control history, its narratives, and its interpretations activated what the Russian scholar Olga Malinova calls 'symbolic politics': 'a set of public activities aimed at the production and promotion/intrusion of certain modes of interpretation of social reality and the struggle for their domination' (Malinova, 2019:87).

The state holds an exclusive role in producing and monitoring symbolic politics. Excessively performative, it includes the creation of new 'state symbols, national holidays, official and unofficial rituals, memory laws' (Malinova, 2019:87). Moreover, performances of symbolic politics often rely on 'simplified narratives that reduce complex and contradictory historical processes to emotionally coloured schemes, which can be easily absorbed. To the extent that such schemes are accepted as "true" and serve as foundations for group identities, they can be considered myths' (Malinova, 2018:37).

In Putin's Russia, the practice of symbolic politics began with the adoption of laws about state symbols, which 'established the three-colour state flag that appealed to the legacy of the Romanov empire and was used by "the democratic forces" as a symbol of their victory during the failed coup d'état in August of 1991, the national anthem based on the "old" melody of the Soviet anthem, and the red flag for the Russian army' (Malinova, 2018:94). These symbols were intended to help Russians forget 'the dark sides of history' and aid Putin's government in creating an image of Russian contentment by focusing people's attention on specifically selected moments in history packaged in attractive, ready-to-be-consumed chunks (94).

Symbolic politics also enabled the state to utilize the performative mechanisms of post-truth, including staged re-enactments, commemorative marches, and glamorous Victory Day parades. Mobilizing symbolic politics, in other words, aided 'the legitimization of power, the justification of political decisions, the search of electoral support, [and] the mobilization of solidarity' (Malinova, 2019:88). It also allowed the government to transform the country's traumatic past into a narrative of glory and to mobilize a new identity based on the age-old us/them binary of nationalism. With Russia's invasion of Ukraine, the ideological work of this propaganda has expanded, with the Russian Orthodox Church firmly aligning itself with the actions of the government, for example.

At the same time, the propaganda's effort to reinstate 'the state monopoly on historical memory and affect provoked a backlash' (Kaluzhsky, 2015). Symbolic politics resurrected the supposedly forgotten Soviet behaviours of doublethink and doublespeak, where in public, people would support the ideology of the state, but in private, they would express very different feelings and attitudes. Commemorations of history produced by private citizens thus began to critique the processes of selecting who is worthy of being remembered and forgotten. Important, because personal memories, experiences, and performative affectations 'undermine foundations of the state symbolic politics', these alternative forms of commemoration occurred in the privacy of peoples' homes and kitchens (Kaluzhsky, 2015).

Despite prohibitive legislation, Russian documentary theatre in general, and Teatr.doc in particular, became 'an effective tool for working with memory and history-related trauma' (Kaluzhsky 2015). It demonstrated that even in totalitarian societies, state-produced ideology can be porous. To explore the impact of the cultural violence produced by Putin's regime, many young artists turned to the Soviet period and discovered that contemporary Russian identity is firmly rooted in the Soviet time: by studying the twentieth-century repressions, they could better understand the newly produced state violence.

The documentary theatre of Anastasia Patlay and Nana Grinstein makes this tendency concrete by giving the victims of history the opportunity to speak. Their work with historical documents – diaries, letters, photographs, and testimonies – centres on physical evidence of injustice and gestures towards what Judith Butler has called the 'bodily speech act' of informed political protest (Butler, 2015). By unearthing the stories of those who have been deliberately committed to oblivion and bringing them to the stage, Patlay and Grinstein effectively challenge the official narratives of nationalism. For Grinstein, it is important not only to establish the historical truth of the document, but also to make old material relevant for today's audiences. When I 'work with archival documents' she explains, 'I interpret them from today's point of view', because for me 'history is not just about today, but also about our future' (Grinstein in Sklez, 2019).

Patlay and Grinstein's biographies position them outside the mainstream. Both artists grew up on the outskirts of the Soviet empire – Patlay in the cosmopolitan city of Tashkent and Grinstein in Baku, the capital of Azerbaijan. Their upbringings formed their artistic tastes and personal politics. Patlay came to Moscow in 1995 to study documentary film, whereas Grinstein moved to the Russian capital to study at the Russian State University of Cinematography (VGIK), with a specialization in screenwriting, and graduated in 1996. Both of them spent years studying theatre directing and dramaturgy.

In common with many racialized migrants in Russia, both artists – although not ethnic minorities – found themselves caught between cultural tides, between mainstream cultural industries and the culture of marginalized subjects, now seeking employment in Moscow. These racialized migrants were often the victims of everyday racism and violence, but they also carried an internalized sense of cosmopolitanism. Living on the outskirts of the empire had made them less dependent on the centre, and for many, notions of home and belonging were inevitably connected to the everyday cosmopolitanism of their upbringings.

This paradox marks Patlay and Grinstein's work. They met in 2012 at Teatr.doc, where they participated in making *Akyn Opera* (directed by Vsevolod Lisovsky), one of a few Russian theatre productions of the period which featured artists-migrants. Patlay and Grinstein's curiosity about the world, which they brought to the project, laid the foundation of their own documentary theatre practice as a mode of resistance to nationalism.

Artistically and politically, Patlay and Grinstein's theatre belongs to the traditions of documentary theatre as pioneered by the creators of Teatr.doc, Elena Gremina and Mikhail Ugarov, in the late 1990s. As free speech began to be censored, by the mid-2000s, Teatr.doc became a place to discuss urgent political issues and seek historical truth. Its objectives were 'to address provocative themes; to explore subjects which were new to the theatre; to cast a fresh eye on reality; to use innovative writing techniques; to remain clear and simple; to prioritize the social dimension of the work; and to challenge the idea of art for art's sake' (Autant-Mathieu, 2020:27). Teatr.doc brought taboo subjects such as 'homosexuality and gender identity issues, youth disaffection, the Orthodox Church and blasphemy, police brutality, prison conditions, political corruption and violence' to the stage (Curtis, 2020:3). In so doing, it rejected elaborate stage settings, used minimalist acting techniques, and turned to the language of the streets, including profanity and non-standard vocabulary, to critique state-sponsored 'monologic narratives about historical issues such as the Stalinist terror' (3).

In 2007, Ugarov published his program article 'Tochka nerazreshimosti', in which he introduced an idea of a 'zero position', when a theatre artist rejects a single artistic and political vision to allow different points of view to be presented simultaneously within the space of a single theatrical event (Ugarov & Shavlovskiy, 2007). With time, this seemingly apolitical standpoint turned into an effective mechanism of political protest, exemplified by Elena Gremina's play *Chas 18/An Hour and Eighteen Minutes* (2010). 'Based largely on documentary sources, the text offered a harrowing account of Sergey Magnitsky's death after his unjust arrest and brutal treatment in police custody, in retaliation for his efforts to protect the commercial and legal interest in Moscow of the British-American businessman Bill Browder' who had exposed fraud and embezzlement by highly placed Russian officials (Curtis, 2020:4). The production was something of a watershed, and Russian documentary theatre entered a phase of active self-politicization as it began to demonstrate that 'private experience can be an alternative testimony to collective memory' (Kaluzhsky, 2015). Among other things, this meant that any documentary performance which deviated from the official version of Russian history became a political statement because of the relationship between the past and the present being tightly controlled by the Russian authorities. The country's past had become highly contested, the focus of 'memory wars' that served various political ends (Sklez in Karas', 2019).

To mobilize their own political project and foreground their ethical concerns, Patlay and Grinstein also turned to historical subjects and documents. They formulated an artistic program – 'document as absence' (Patlay & Grinstein, 2020) – based on the acknowledgement of fundamental uncertainties around access to and interpretation of history. They identified five steps of engagement with a document – anticipation of discovery, temporal distancing, counterpoint, emptiness, and actualization of the material – vital to the making of documentary theatre projects based on historical events and materials (155). Each of these steps registers the artist's inability to fully capture historical truth, and the model outlines her journey from the moment she locates a document, which produces anticipation or artistic promise (step one), to acknowledgement of temporal distancing and the existence of contextual gaps in the material (step two). This journey aligns with Walter Benjamin's reading of history as a snapshot of memory that appears before our eyes only at a moment of danger (Benjamin, 2003:396). Such realization invites the dramaturgical tactic of counterpoint (step three).

Based on Brechtian techniques of fragmentation and montage, counterpoint involves the juxtaposition of evidence when a new historical document is inserted into the scene. This principle also allows the artist to reveal hidden historical truths that might not be immediately accessible via a single document. In a country that continually supresses political movements and free speech, juxtaposing one piece of evidence with another helps to illuminate historical injustice and to create urgent messages about the present.

Emptiness (step four) refers to the responsibility of the spectator to fill the gaps in historical information, which is either not in the documents or omitted by the artists. Like Brecht, Grinstein and Patlay seek to acknowledge gaps and erasures in history, to avoid imposing any single interpretation of the past, and to provide spectators with intellectual stimulation in theatre. This expectation of labour – from the artist, who tries to avoid interpretation, to the spectator, who is obliged to make an intellectual effort – is the element of political resistance Grinstein and Patlay activate in their work.

The final step of the document as an absence model is historical actualization of the material. This once again echoes Benjamin's view of the historian's political responsibility. For Benjamin, the true (materialist) historian writes about the past from their own temporal position, from which history appears not as 'the "eternal" image of the past', but 'a unique experience with the past' (Benjamin, 2003:396). As Patlay and Grinstein explain, the effect of absence serves as a special emotional resource of documentary theatre and helps spectators to engage with the document. Such absences are invitations for the audience to 'suffer' – that is, they force the audience to attempt 'to better understand what this absence or silence means' (Patlay & Grinstein, 2020:163).

For Russian audiences, who are more familiar with representational theatre and for whom Brechtian devices of alienation remain rather foreign, working on empathy through intellect is a new experience. It encourages critical political thinking and personal resistance. To further evidence this statement, I now turn to Patlay and Grinstein's 2022 project, *Memoria*.

Memoria opened on 9 February 2022, two weeks before the Russian invasion of Ukraine. It was the last production Patlay and Grinstein presented in Moscow before their exile to Spain and Germany respectively, and it was the last project produced by the Meyerhold Theatre Centre (TSIM) before its closure in March 2022.[3] *Memoria* tells the story of the German actress Carola Neher, who died in the NKVD prison camp in 1942, alongside the tale of the closure of Memorial, the Russian human rights organization that was a co-recipient of the 2022 Noble Peace Prize. *Memoria*'s subject matter, its political overtones, and its disappearance from the repertoire serve as further evidence of the oppressive practices of Putin's regime.

The work on this play went through several stages: its first 2018 version was entitled *Carola Neher: Bruchnaya rol'/ Carola Neher: The Trouser Part*, presented by the human rights organization International Memorial as part of the exhibit 'The Theatre of Carola Neher's Life', which was dedicated to the famous German actress who perished in the Soviet camps. Thanks to Irina Shcherbakova, head of the International Memorial's outreach programmes and curator of the exhibition, Patlay and Grinstein received access to the archives and focused their story solely on Neher's life and death.

Neher was Brecht's favorite collaborator, the first to play the role of Polly Peachum in his *The Threepenny Opera*, 'a symbol of women's emancipation and a leading figure among Berlin intellectuals' (Pal'veleva, 2022). When Hitler came to power, Neher and her husband, Anatol Becker, decided to seek asylum in the USSR. Becker was accused of espionage in 1936 and killed in 1937, while Neher was arrested and died of typhus in 1942 in the Sol-Ilezk transit camp. Their son, Georg, spent his childhood in Soviet orphanages unaware of his parents' fate. Neher was rehabilitated in 1959, but her story resurfaced due only to the efforts of

[3] After Elena Kovalskaya, TSIM's managing director, publicly condemned Putin's government for its military aggression and stepped down from her position, *Memoria* was instantly taken off the repertoire, while TSIM itself was closed.

Irina Shcherbakova. Shcherbakova collected the testimonies of former Soviet prisoners, including those who met Neher. She also found Neher's correspondence with the Soviet authorities in which the actress sought information about her son. In the 1990s, Shcherbakova invited Georg to visit Russia and learn the truth about his mother's death. Shcherbakova's research and recollections about her work provided the second narrative layer of the play and its new version, now entitled *Memoria*.

The history of creation and dismantling of the human rights organization Memorial was used to create a third historical layer in the work, which thus made explicit the connections between Stalin's purges and Putin's political oppression. Founded in January 1989, Memorial was created to seek justice for the victims of the Stalinist regime. With time it turned into a precious archive of alternative Soviet history, radically different from the glorified narrative constructed by Putin's propaganda. In 2012, after the Russian government passed the so-called Foreign Agents Law (The State Duma, 2012), Memorial was labelled a foreign agent and thus found itself under increased scrutiny. The Russian Ministry of Justice declared the Russian branch of Memorial a foreign agent on 21 July 2014. In 2016, it extended this label to Memorial International. On 28 December 2021, the Supreme Court of Russia recommended Memorial close for violations of the Foreign Agents Law and in April 2022, Memorial was fully shut down.

The testimonies of Memorial's founders and speeches of Mikhail Gorbachev and Andrey Sakharov, as well as transcripts from the December 2021 court proceedings, were incorporated into *Memoria*'s final script. Placing Carola Neher's personal story and the history of making and dismantling of Memorial next to each other established continuity of totalitarian and oppressive practices in modern Russia. More specifically, in the play, 'it became difficult to distinguish between the language of a modern trial and that of the old documents. They exhibit similar stylistic patterns and the same measure of shameless absurdity' (Patlay in Pal'veleva, 2022). The contemporary political context enhanced the significance of Neher's fate. *Memoria* positioned itself in opposition to the state as the institute of punishment and violence (see Figures 9, 10, and 11).

The title, *Memoria*, carries particular symbolism. The word comes from Latin and in its primary meaning is directly linked to historical commemoration, as well as the art of rhetoric and lamentation. This symbolism is reflected in the staging:

> The semi-darkness of the performance space ... instantly moves spectators out from the comfort of their everyday lives and places them into a dense historical-mythological realm ... Staggered boots, as if they have been taken from the feet of GULAG prisoners, are placed on the floor next to the old tape recorders that reproduce testimonies of historical witnesses ... This is a symbolic space of the internal prison to which the Stalinist dictatorship condemns its victims, a space of spiritual torture and testing. (Kolyazin, 2022)

Figure 9 *Memoria*. TSIM. February 9, 2022; Photo by Katya Kraeva. With Mikhail Shamkov as Brecht, Yasmina Omerovich as Carola, and Irina Savitcova as Shcherbakova.

Figure 10 *Memoria*. TSIM. February 9, 2022; Photo by Katya Kraeva. With Mikhail Shamkov as Brecht, Yasmina Omerovich as Carola, and Irina Savitcova as Shcherbakova.

Figure 11 *Memoria*. TSIM. February 9, 2022; Photo by Katya Kraeva. With Mikhail Shamkov as Brecht, Yasmina Omerovich as Carola, and Irina Savitcova as Shcherbakova.

Positioned at the junction of fiction and documentary, *Memoria* brings historical and contemporary figures into the spotlight. For example, Grinstein inserted Brecht's anti-fascist and anti-war poems into the text, making them *Memoria*'s political songs. When Neher's life becomes unbearable, she also turns to Brecht and recites her lines from *The Threepenny Opera*. In this way, Brecht appears in the script 'personally', as someone whose attitude to the Soviet Union and to Stalin were highly ambiguous. In addition to documentary evidence from the Memorial trial, Grinstein includes social media discussions, thus creating a palimpsest of historical speeches, fictional texts, poetry, trial records, and private posts, which together generate a new sense of historical and dramaturgical truth.

To activate the political consciousness of the young actors involved, Patlay asked them to engage in extensive research on Stalinist purges and the GULAG. It was important for Patlay to ensure the actors felt personally connected to the historical material. At the same time, as narrators of this history, they needed to allow Neher, Brecht, and the other historical figures to speak for themselves. Consequently, in another nod to Brecht, 'the actors were to remain as themselves, without falling into any psychological representation' (Patlay & Grinstein, 2022). The result was striking.

The young performers, who had no direct connection to the historical period they portrayed, created new historical evidence on stage. Using the headphone-verbatim technique, in which 'the actor listens to the historical recording through headphones and repeats the words aloud', each performer served as a 'transmitter not an interpreter' of historical truth (Patlay & Grinstein, 2022). *Memoria*'s performers thus became what Freddie Rokem has described as 'hyper-historians' able to channel the energy of a historical document to their audiences (2000:13). In common with Brecht's theatre, this approach was intended to inform and to implicate *Memoria*'s spectators in the re-enactment of history, thus encouraging them to view the past and present critically and to look beyond the state's glossy representations of history. For this reason, when *Memoria* was removed from the repertoire, it became a special piece of historical evidence testifying to the dangerous and oppressive practices of recurring totalitarianism in the Russian context. The closure reinforced Patlay and Grinstein's position as political activists.

4 Staging the Other: Contesting Nationalism

Since the collapse of the Soviet Union, Russian theatre and performance artists have attempted to confront the problematic heritage of their country and its growing nationalist tendencies. Questioning of the Soviet totalitarian past, systemic and everyday racism, misogyny, and religious intolerance marks the work of the generation of theatre makers who emerged in Russia in the early 2000s. In this section, I examine methodologies of 'decolonial aestheSis' as a strategy for myth-breaking in the context of Russian nationalism's performative discourses and practices (Tlostanova, 2019). I focus on the work of post--Soviet non-Russian racialized artists who use performance to stage their multiple cultural, ethnic, linguistic, and religious identities.

My first example is Nuria Fatykhova's *Avazlar* (November 2020–June 2021) which was produced by Kazan Theatre Platform MOÑ and aims to resurrect the Tatar language through participatory performance, thereby contesting the totalizing and colonizing narratives and practices of Russian nationalism. My second case study is the work of Olzhas Zhanaidarov, a Kazakh-Russian writer. His debut play, *Dzhut* (2013), depicts the ordeals of Soviet Kazakhs during the 1930s famine (*dzhut*) in order to demonstrate how the projects of Soviet colonization and migration intersect.

Dzhut dismantles the myth of Soviet republics living happily in peace and equality under the protection of Russia, the mother of all nations, and Stalin, their father. Zhanaidarov's 2015 play *Magazine/Store* continues this argument. Although set in Putin's Russia, it tells the story of a young Kazakh woman,

Karlygash, who comes to Moscow to seek employment but falls victim to organized crime. A racialized migrant in Moscow and an unmarried woman, Karlygash is hired as a salesperson in the local grocery store run by Ziyash, a racialized migrant herself. Ziyash has found a way to integrate. Under the protection of the local police, she keeps her female migrant workers in slavery. By revealing the multiple layers of corruption and abuse many racialized migrants experience, Zhanaidarov condemns systemic racism and oppression. He also speaks to issues of patriarchy as deeply engrained within Kazakh traditional culture, and to the problems of illegal migration, exploitation, and violence as practised by the Russian authorities, law enforcement, and individuals.

Scholars tell two competing stories about the making of Russia. Alexander Etkind usefully describes them as one that concerns 'a great country that competes successfully, though unevenly, with other European powers, produces brilliant literature, and stages unprecedented social experiments' and another 'of economic backwardness, unbridled violence, misery, illiteracy, despair, and collapse' (Etkind, 2011:1). Both narratives present Russia as an empire expanding its territories via external colonialism and as colonizing non-ethnic Russians who live in its own territories in a gesture best described as internal colonialism. For centuries, these multidirectional processes of colonization defined the workings of the Russian state, while the peoples of the empire 'developed anti-imperial, nationalist ideas in response' (Etkind, 2011:2). Both tendencies find special echoing in the nationalist project of Putin's Russia.

The beginnings of the Russian empire date to the Muscovy period (between the early fourteenth and eighteenth centuries), when expanding territories and conversion to Orthodox Christianity served as major strategies of Russian nation-building. By the mid-nineteenth century, it was a nationality policy or 'Russification' that became the leading device of Russian colonization (Suny, 2001:41–54). To 'regulate the ethno-cultural status quo', the policy presupposed assimilation, acculturation, and integration of ethnic groups within the cultural, economic, and social practices of the empire. As a result, while ethnic minorities surrendered economic and political privileges and lost territorial autonomy, ethnic Russians accumulated new territorial, cultural, and linguistic privileges (Pearson, 1989:94). At the same time, the question of ethnicity was not fully articulated by the empire builders who still used Orthodox Christianity as the leading doctrine of Russification. This resulted in an offensive against the churches of the minority groups that populated Russian territories (Pearson, 1989:94).

Russian conservatism actively developed during the rule of Tsar Nicholas I, who fathered the ideology of 'Official Nationality' to 'counter Western

European liberalism and emphasize Russia's distinctiveness' (Robinson, 2019:45). Count Sergey Uvarov was to implement this ideology by introducing reforms to the educational system and 'instill within it a new "national" spirit' (45). He summed up his reform in the official slogan 'Orthodoxy, Autocracy, Nationality', which, according to Uvarov, was to 'form the distinctive character of Russia' and serve as 'the basis of the moral education of Russia's youth' – that is, 'the anchor of our salvation' (Ugarov in Robinson, 2019:45).

The slogan 'emphasised the close ties between the tsar and the people, a bond said to go back to Muscovy' (Suny, 2001:47). These developments were complemented by 'Russianization' practices, which involved 'the increased hegemony of Russian language, culture, and institutions' (Pearson, 1989:89). Recognition of the Russian language as the official language of state governance, public speech, and education marked Russia's 'linguistic imperialism', with the authorities imposing restrictions on the use of minority languages in the provincial administrations and courts (95). Bilingualism, knowledge of one's native language and Russian, became a special condition for long-term employment in the territories occupied by the country's minorities. Across the empire, ethnic Russians enjoyed privileged access to education and employment, while the state created a system of quotas for minorities, specifically Jews, preventing them from fully integrating into civic society.

The final step in the building of the empire was Russia's annexation of the territories that historically belonged to others. Poles and Finns were made special targets of annexation, with many people driven away from their homes and communities. This re-territorialization destroyed the traditional lifestyles of many groups and forced them to consider emigration. Thus, by the time of the 1917 Bolshevik Revolution, the empire had successfully implemented its nationality policy and laid the foundation for the further assimilation and acculturation of ethnic groups in the Soviet era.

When the Bolsheviks came to power, they proclaimed the equality of all groups and nationalities, or what Terry Martin calls the 'Soviet affirmative action policy' (Martin, 2001:67). Both Lenin and Stalin attacked tsarism for its oppression of the minorities. They condemned the great Russian chauvinism and openly positioned themselves against its colonizing practices. In March 1919, Lenin urged the leaders of the new state to consider the right of national self-determination for each republic and territory within the new Soviet state. Attracting the populations of Muslim countries in the East and Slavic nations in the West was Bolsheviks' major goal. It resulted in the 'annexation of Poland's large Ukrainian population,' and its later recolonization (72). In 1923, Soviet Russia proclaimed the formation of 'national territories, national languages, national elites, and national cultures' integral to the state, with some minorities receiving 'extraterritorial rights to govern their own cultural affairs' (73). This policy resulted in 'a grandiose pyramid of national Soviets consisting of thousands of national territories of varying size' and so required educating new national elites in their national languages (73). As a gesture of perceived decolonialization, the state called for the nationalization of peoples' cultural practices and native languages with the aim of converting them into loyal Soviet citizens.

During the early part of Stalin's rule, 'Soviet policy systematically promoted the distinctive national identity and national self-consciousness of its non-Russian populations' (Martin, 2001:74). It encouraged national elites to use national languages and promoted symbolic markers of national identity, including national arts, culture, and customs. Yet, wary of the rise of national elites and their calls for independence, Stalin and his government slowly began to abandon this policy. Russians, their language, and their cultural and social practices were again recognized as dominant across the entire Soviet population. As Martin notes, this 'new principle of Soviet unity was represented by the metaphor of "Friendship of the Peoples"' (81). Forged by the Russians, it was presented as a 'supranational imagined community for the multi-ethnic Soviet people' and a brand of Stalin's Internationalism, which was held together by Russian glue and maintained its hold on the country until the late 1980s (81).

Gregory Alexandrov's 1936 film *Circus* speaks directly to the Friendship of the Peoples myth as mobilized by the affirmative action policy. Influenced by American musicals, *Circus* is an excellent example of Soviet propaganda. It stages a utopian image of a strong, friendly, and all-encompassing country of workers, with all ethnic groups united under the leadership of Russia. *Circus* tells a story of Marion Dixon, an American circus artist played by the 1930s Soviet film star Lubov' Orlova, who after having an illegitimate black son, must escape American racism. She ends up in the Soviet Union as the star of the Moscow circus.

Feeling safe and in love in Soviet Russia, Marion decides to stay there. However, her German manager, Franz von Kneishitz, threatens to reveal her secret. In the film's climatic scene, Kneishitz tries to incriminate Marion by presenting her black baby to the Muscovites. To his surprise, the Soviet citizens take Marion's side. They snatch the boy from his evil hands and return him to his mother. As the people pass the boy from one person to the next, they sing a lullaby and as the camera moves from one face to the next, the viewer is presented with a perfect scene of Soviet equality and diversity: people of different cultures and ethnicities, representatives of the Soviet republics, willingly and happily sing a Russian lullaby in Russian, Ukrainian, Yiddish, Uzbek, and Georgian to a black child. A black man wearing a Soviet naval officer's uniform completes the image, as the circus' Russian director tells Kneishitz that Soviet people love all children, regardless of race.

The film closes with the ultimate image of Soviet propaganda. The characters are transported to Red Square, as Marion, her black son, and her Soviet lover march into their bright future. 'Song about the Motherland', which they sing together and which serves as the ideological vertebrae of the film, further reinforces the idea of Soviet internationalism. The white of the characters' uniforms and the red of the Soviet flags support this image of totalitarian bliss. Here the individual, with her personal aspirations, wishes, and dreams, is glossed over in order to underscore the myth of collective happiness. Although *Circus* belongs to Soviet propaganda, it holds a symbolic place in the performative iconography of Russian nationalism, and as such it continues to serve as an idealized symbolic backdrop against which today's work of decolonization, resistance, and protest can be projected.

The collapse of the Soviet Union in 1991 marked the end of the affirmative action policy, with Mikhail Gorbachev aspiring to turn the 'Soviet empire into a post-Soviet national, somewhat democratic and partly legal state' (Pastukhov, 2022). Yeltsin's coming to power signalled a return to the nationalist agenda, which returned the country to its pre-Soviet imperial form. Yet it also faced a kind of grassroots decolonization, with the former Soviet republics embarking on their own paths of self-determination and nationalism. When Putin came to power, his publicists turned to the slogan 'Great Russia' to present Putin as a leader capable of uniting a disintegrating Russian state and of satisfying 'the competing expectations and interests of diverse domestic constituencies' (Burrett, 2020:495).

In his 2000 New Year's address, Putin declared Orthodoxy the spiritual core of the state, effectively binding it to all ethnic Russians. Starting with his 2013 appearance at the Valdai Club, Putin 'emphasised the importance of identity in the spiritual, cultural and national senses, and seriously called for restoring a cultural code with links to Russian national tradition and history' (Jonson, 2018:14). In December 2014, after Russia annexed Crimea, he signed a presidential decree entitled 'Foundations for a New State Cultural Policy', which presented Russia as 'a unique civilization beyond the categories of "West" and "East" but uniting these two worlds' (19). The decree distinguished Russia from Western civilization and embraced 'traditional Russian values' including 'national, patriotic and religious ones', rooted in the moral code of Orthodox Christianity as well as the beliefs of 'other religions and non-Russian ethnic groups on Russian territory' (Jonson, 2018:19). Its major objective was 'to preserve the identity of the Russian civilization and its specific values', with the state acting as 'the regulator of the system of cultural institutions' (Jonson, 2018:19). Putin quickly adopted this divisive rhetoric. The 2014 crisis in Ukraine gave him 'the perfect opportunity to ignite nationalist sentiments on which to build a new base of anti-Western support for his leadership' (Burrett, 2020:498). The 2022 invasion of Ukraine allowed the Russian government to escalate the rhetoric of nationalism and embrace territorial imperialism.

From a Western perspective, however, Russia appeared a kind of second-class empire. It was seen as irrational, subaltern, archaic, and thus difficult to comprehend. In relation to its natural resources, literature, and arts, it was recognized only as a 'producing culture', a perspective that irritated Putin and his team (Tlostanova, 2015:50). For the racialized subjects of Russia, the rise of Putin's nationalism brought new forms of internal colonization. For Madina Tlostanova, 'the post-Soviet space emerge[d] as marked with many silences and omissions, unspoken resentments and continued insults between Russian and non-Russian, secondary European and non-European subjects. The latter [were] often even less aware of their discrimination and not ready to formulate their own stance' (51).

Yet it was also time for ethnic minorities to challenge Putin's nationalist project, with performing arts at the avant-garde of the post-Soviet decolonization. Tlostanova defines 'decolonial aestheSis' as a methodology for resistance to Putin's nationalism through art (Tlostanova, 2019:102). A critique of postcoloniality, her strategy 'contributes to making visible decolonial subjectivities at the confluence of popular practices of re-existence' (Mignolo & Vazquez, 2013). Thought of as not merely an object of inquiry, but as the endured lived condition from which a decolonial artist speaks, decolonial aestheSis aims to publicly reinstate people whose affective experiences 'have been seen as dangerous' and who have been consequently silenced and erased from previous historical accounts' (Tlostanova, 2019:103).

Tlostanova explains that 'in decolonial interpretations, the Soviet past and post-Soviet present are seen as complex intersectional conglomerates of ideology, ethnic racial, gender, religious, colonial, indigenous and other factors instead of homogenous ideological constructs' (102). Performance art has proved an effective platform for decolonial aestheSis, and for the emergence of post-Soviet decoloniality and activist expressions, particularly for the work of post-Soviet artists coming from 'the non-European ex-colonies of the USSR' (103). Tlostanova emphasises how far these.

> Artists were weary of the prescribed Soviet aesthetic models, including those created specifically for the ethnic-national others, and uneasy about simply emulating Western trends. They attempted to decolonise their aesthesis in turning to forgotten native models of perception censored during the Soviet time and dismissed as outdated in the only remaining global neoliberal modernity after 1989 (Tlostanova, 2019:103).

At the present time, these artists utilize strategies for 'regenerating and re-futuring' their lived experiences via engagement with 'forgotten native sounds, tastes and odours', practices of 'geo-body storytelling', the use of 'parody, mimicry, chiasmus, overlay, exaggerated nostalgia, deconstruction and creolisation of the previous official aesthetic norms and rules of Soviet modernity' (103). Reclaiming the lost languages, memories, and histories of decolonised subjects can lead to 'the resurgence of native cosmologies and local histories vis-à-vis modernity', and its homogenizing discourses (100). Born in the ruins of empire and often on its geographical margins, these politically aware non-ethnic Russian artists challenge the discourses and practices of Putin's nationalism. Their work excavates the Soviet past, its myths of internationalism and tolerance, but also the persistence of systemic and everyday racism, misogyny, and religious intolerance. They interrogate their multiple cultural, ethnic, linguistic, and religious legacies, using performance to investigate histories of forced uprooting, loss of religion and cultural practices, and native languages. The reclamation of heritage, especially language, typically drives these artistic projects. In the next section, I explore one case study in detail.

The Russian constitution recognizes Russian 'as the state language of the entire country' but also 'guarantees all its peoples the right to preserve their native language and to create the conditions for its study and development' (Arutyunova & Zamyatin, 2021:833). Education plays a major role in language preservation, with many autonomous republics providing mandatory instruction in titular ethnic languages to both native and non-native Russian speakers. However, when a 2018 federal law on language and education was introduced, all language instruction of titular ethnic languages in Russia and its regions was made optional except for Russian itself (The State Duma, 2018). The teaching of titular ethnic languages essentially became extracurricular.

This change created circumstances in which the state was able to promote Russian linguistic and cultural identity over those of indigenous subjects living in these regions. This issue has become particularly problematic in the Republic of Tatarstan, where many intellectuals, cultural activists, and artists expressed their dissatisfaction with the new law and mobilized cultural initiatives to help preserve the Tatar language (Arutyunova & Zamyatin, 2021:841–3). The experimental Theatre Platform MOÑ in Kazan was the centre for one such practice. It aimed both to reclaim the Tatar language as the major vehicle of communication in Tatarstan, and to turn it into a tool for political resistance and decolonial dissent.

MOÑ opened in autumn 2020 at the National Library of Tatarstan, in Kazan, with the support and encouragement of the Meyerhold Theatre Center (TSIM) in Moscow, which spearheaded initiatives in decolonization and decentralization and supported the creation of independent centers and venues across Russia. With no permanent acting company, MOÑ is run by a team of curators who encourage projects under the banner 'theatre of the townspeople'. Privileging experimental, immersive, and participatory projects, MOÑ also seeks to ensure the active involvement of non-professional performers. It supports initiatives in decentralization to reflect multiple cultural, linguistic, and historical connections in which the culture of a multi-ethnic and cosmopolitan city of Kazan is rooted.

One of MOÑ's inaugural projects, *Avazlar*, was based on participants' slow reading of historical texts written by ordinary Tatar citizens. The texts were compiled by the political journalist Nuria Fatykhova, the ethnographer Alfrid Bustanov, and a group of scholars of Tatar history from Kazan. Presented on three consecutive evenings, the project also featured texts from public donations: the letters, diaries, and poetry of ordinary Tatars donated in response to an open call.

For the creators of *Avazlar*, its immersive and durational nature was key. The company believed that reading old Tatar texts in public constitutes a decolonizing gesture: it meant to reclaim the use of Tatar language on the territory of the Russian Federation traditionally inhabited by the indigenous Tatar people. The readings invited participants to immerse themselves in the lost world of the past, to encounter Tatar people, who were historically displaced by the colonizing practices of Russia, and to materialize them in the contemporary moment. Listening to the texts being read aloud in Tatar also served as an invitation to bridge the time/space continuum that separates people from their past, to challenge their parents' stories and beliefs, and to question their own identities. Although these readings took place in Tatar, the discussions and talkbacks were held in Tatar and Russian with simultaneous translations (see Figures 12, 13, and 14).

For Nuria Fatykhova, the curator of the project, making *Avazlar* was a highly personal endeavour designed to help her respond to the question: what does it mean to be a Tatar woman today? Questions of identity have obviously been on the forefront of Fatykhova's thinking, since she identifies as a 'Tatar-woman from Moscow' (Fatykhova, 2020a). Born in Uzbekistan, Fatykhova comes from a family that lived in special resettlements in the Urals, to where they had been deported in the 1930s, after the dekulakization period[4]. An ethnic Tatar,

[4] *Dekulakization* refers to the forced expropriation of private properties and farmland from the prosperous peasants and their families initiated by the Soviet authorities. It included arrests, deportations, and executions of millions of *kulaks*.

Figure 12 *Avazlar*. MOÑ, November 2020, Photo by Zoe Ruter, with Nyria Fatykhova and performance participants.

Figure 13 *Avazlar*. MOÑ, November 2020, Photo by Zoe Ruter, with Nyria Fatykhova and performance participants.

Fatykhova is an example of a decolonial subject who speaks from the lived and embodied experience of colonization and uprooting. By her own account, she 'grew up in an urban Russianised family, spoke no Tatar at home, and is now traveling around the world in search for her Tatar identity' (Fatykhova, 2020a). Making *Avazlar* was an opportunity for Fatykhova to reclaim her heritage, and

Figure 14 *Avazlar*. MOÑ, November 2020, Photo by Zoe Ruter, with Nyria Fatykhova and performance participants.

also to come to terms with the tragic history of her family and her people, who were victims of the Soviet colonization project in Tatarstan.

As was typically the case, the Soviet colonization of Tatarstan relied on the uprooting of people through forced displacement, the prohibition of religious practices, and a programme of linguistic assimilation which resulted in Tatars forgetting their own language. As a result, currently Russian Tatars often do not live on their land, practise their religion, or speak their language. Nonetheless, they remain visible minorities, out of place, Othered, and unprotected from the racism directed against them.

This history created a sense of internal displacement and identity crisis. Interested in issues of social justice, cultural memory, gender and education, anti-discrimination, ethics, and freedom of speech, Fatykhova wrote extensively on these subjects. It was the publication of Guzel Yakhina's best-selling novel *Zuleikha Opens Her Eyes* (2015), however, and the subsequent TV mini-series (2020) featuring the famous Moscow actress Chulpan Khamatova, an ethnic Tatar herself, that proved a turning point. Fatykhova realized the time had come to publicly embrace her own ethnic and cultural identity, even if to understand what it means to be Tatar today would become a life-defining task.

The action of Yakhina's novel begins in a small Tatar village, in 1930, at the start of the dekulakization and social cleansing that lasted until 1933. In the novel, Zuleikha is married to a *kulak* who is eventually killed by communists, and so she is forced into exile. On her journey to the penal colony on Angara River in Siberia, she meets a doctor, an avant-garde painter, representatives of Russian intelligentsia, and fellow peasants, all victims of the purges. To a Muslim Tatar woman, however, the journey presents additional obstacles. Raised in a strict household, deeply religious, and with no knowledge of the Russian language, to survive the journey Zuleikha is forced to abandon all of her traditions.

The book raises difficult questions about personal honour and physical survival as they relate to a Muslim Tatar woman. It explores what it means for someone like Zuleikha to 'open her eyes', a metaphor for self-discovery as much as discovery of the world. The book concludes with the image of Zuleikha, a survivor who despite the horrors of deportation has been able to give birth to and raise a child, and even find personal satisfaction, if not dignity, in her position as chief hunter in the unit created by the exiled prisoners in the penal colony of Semruk.

Although the book received the Yasnaya Polyana Literary Award and the Big Book Award in 2015, its reception was mixed and it reignited debates about Tatar identity and nationalism. Tatar critics attacked the book for its 'crudely stylised image of Tatar culture', complaining 'it was marketed as an example of a new Tatar national literature', while the descendants of the victims 'critiqued the novel for embellishment of the Kulak settlements' (Fatykhova, 2020b). Russian conservatives, including Maxim Suraikin, the chairman of the Communists of Russia Party, also expressed concern. For Suraikin, the book aimed to 'discredit the Soviet period and our citizens'. Albir Hazrat, the head of the Spiritual Assembly of Muslims of Russia, found the representation of Russian muftis as political prisoners unacceptable (Goncharov, 2020).

Fatykhova was also among those critics who voiced concerns about the book. Her criticism was directed at Yakhina's mythologizing of the history of Tatar colonization. Although Yakhina claims the novel is based on the experiences of her own grandmother, for Fatykhova, 'the book presents us with a collective image of a "dreary" and "cruel" Tatar resisting Soviet civilisation' (Fatykhova, 2020b). The narrative of colonization goes hand in hand with orientalism and presentation of the female body as oversexualized and exoticized. The novel also continues a tradition of colonial literature in assigning 'a male other a higher status than the female one' (Fatykhova, 2020b).

Yakhina describes the relationships between the Tatar and the Soviet worlds within this system of colonial interdependencies as a proverbial West-East or master-slave dichotomy. In this instance, in Fatykhova's reading, 'the slave is passive, a sullen Other, who must be tamed or forced into a normative Western subject', and so the novel becomes an example of cultural tokenism (Fatykhova, 2020b). Zuleikha's feminist journey from the wife of an abusive religious man, a mere shadow and tool, to a person in her own right who is free to choose her mate, turns into a melodrama of emotional speculation from the repertoire of a 'neostalinist folklore' (Fatykhova, 2020b). Yet, for Fatykhova, despite

Yakhina's novel being 'a replica of Russia's political consciousness and its imperial complexes,' its value is in gesturing towards meaningful tactics of decolonization (2020b). The novel invites Tatar people to recognize themselves as unique, to claim their rights to a voice, and 'to break out of the trap of imperial logic' (2020b).

To begin her personal journey of decolonization, Fatykhova turned away from the novel towards her own history as a Tatar woman, deeply rooted in the life stories of her ancestors. One of the prominent voices that emerges in *Avazlar* is that of her great-grandmother Mukhtar'yama, a well-educated Muslim woman from a Tatar village, who fell victim to dekulakization when her family was relocated to Magnitogorsk in the southern Urals. To preserve family traditions and language, Mukhtar'yama kept a diary, wrote letters to her relatives in Tatarstan, and composed poetry. These writings are full of personal nostalgia and lyricism, but also pain. Restoring Mukhtar'yama's diary became Fatykhova's personal act of decolonization. Before working on *Avazlar*, she could not call herself a Tatar because she simply did not know what the word meant. The story of her great-grandmother, whose diary was written in Arabic, which Fatykhova could not fully decipher, brought meaning to the concept. Fatykhova learned that even in exile, her great grandmother continued her silent project of resistance. To protect her identity as a Muslim and as a Tatar, Mukhtar'yama wrote down important dates, recorded family recipes, and described cultural customs, so to make sure tradition lived on in her household. She never became a truly Soviet woman.

The neocolonialism of Putin's Russia stands on the same ground as the unatoned crimes of Stalinism. While this domestic history and practice of resistance seems to be forgotten or is re-mythologized via orientalist tropes, the colonizer continues to maintain a superiority complex towards subaltern people, which manifests in a desire to lump the 'little peoples' together into a mysterious and undeveloped Orient. *Avazlar* emerges against this political backdrop, in response to a 'flourishing of neo-Stalinism' and Putin's making the Russian language the 'natural spiritual framework of a multinational country' (Fatykhova, 2020b). To fight this new nationalism, Fatykhova calls for the reclamation of the Tatar language. As she explains, many Tatars experience a 'language gap between generations', they cannot know or understand what their grandparents thought, because they simply do not know their language (2020b). An additional difficulty is that, in its written form, Tatar changed alphabets several times. *Avazlar* builds on this complexity. Its texts contain passages written in Arabic, Latin, and Cyrillic and are compiled chronologically to follow the history of the region and the loss of its language.

Chronology is important, as is tempo. Fatykhova describes her project as a documentary performance rooted in theatricality. The participants are invited to perform a slow reading of the texts, a technique of mourning based on people naming things, speaking the sounds of the language, and listening. The goal is to learn how to make sounds and to hear voices: 'we wanted our throat, our ligaments, our tongue to become an instrument for the voices of those people, whom history and we ourselves had pushed away' (Fatykhova, 2020b). Participants, who are bilingual speakers of Russian and Tatar, are also invited to engage in translation. Every Russian text is translated into Tatar. Even if only a symbolic gesture, this process of translation is important because to reclaim a lost language this language must be given a special status in the sphere of communication.

To reinforce the effect of collective reclaiming and repossession of the language, the project unfolds in three different spatial locations between which participants move. This effect of spatial/temporal simultaneity generates a sense of a new collectivity, which in turn enhances the affective power of the theatrical encounter/event. This is not to suggest that the individual is subsumed into the collective. For Fatykhova, there is no one way to identify as Tatar. People's personal histories and the stories of their families, located within the monumental narratives of empire, determine their responses and positionality. In this regard, Tlostanova's notion of 'pluriversality' (Fry and Tlostanova, 2021:69) has helped Fatykhova anchor her work emotionally and politically. For Tlostanova, when one's biography, geography, and lived knowledge are inseparable, universality is replaced by pluriversality (Fry and Tlostanova, 2021:69–71). The identities of post-Soviet people have long been intertwined such that for decolonial subjects, including Fatykhova herself, pluriversality becomes the norm. 'I am not only a Tatar, only a post-Soviet woman, only a Russian', Fatykhova writes, 'I have my memory and my knowledge, but I also have a lot of local and global identities . . . It is no longer possible to squeeze me into a single concept, whether I am a post-Soviet person or a person from Putin's time' (Fatykhova, 2020b). For post-Soviet Tatars of multiple identities, protection of the Tatar language is nevertheless a major act of decolonization and resistance to Putin's nationalism.

Together with colonization, external and internal migration was a crucial factor in the growth of the Russian empire. From Peter the Great to Stalin, the question of how to develop 'the fertile lands in the Central European part of the empire along the Volga River and stimulate agricultural development' remained central (Ivakhnuk, 2009:4). Internal migration was restricted by serfdom, so for two centuries, skilled European migrants relocated to Russia, where they were offered privileges 'such as tax relief, freedom of conscience, and exemption from military service' (4). Internal migration became possible only in the late nineteenth century when serfdom was abolished and Russian peasants started moving around the country.

In time, their multiple migrations became 'a major resource of colonization of the Empire's margins' (Ivakhnuk, 2009:4). During the Soviet period, patterns of internal migration changed. On one hand, migration was imposed from the top down through forced displacement of entire populations and groups. On the other hand, it was driven by employment, as people 'moved to large-scale construction and industrial sites within the rigidly organised labor recruitment system' (7). Economic migrants were expected to settle in the remote parts of the Soviet empire, so their relocation was stimulated by financial incentives, including 'a traveling allowance, regional wage increments, early retirement and a higher pension, accommodation, annual paid vacation with transport fares covered by the state, free vouchers to a health resort and so on' (7). In 1932, a new system of population control was introduced in which the registration 'of the passport holder at a specific address (*propiska*)' was formally legalized (5).[5] This seriously limited people's movement across the country. Yet passport and *propiska* were privileges of the urban populations, while peasants (*kolkhozniki*) often did not hold a passport and until 1974 'had no right to move even within the borders of the administrative unit (province) where they lived' (5).

The collapse of the Soviet Union forced newly emerged independent states to reconsider migration rules. Effectively, most migration took place within or between the former Soviet republics, so 'migration from Russia to Kazakhstan or from one Russian oblast (province) to another was regulated by the same rules' (Ivakhnyuk, 2009:11). Drivers and patterns of internal migration also changed. Most post-Soviet migration was marked by economic necessity, with some caused by the repatriation of ethnic groups to their places of origin. Individuals who took on the functions of new merchants, the so-called *chelnoks*, constituted a second group of internal migrants. In the 1990s, *chelnoks* transported goods before official transport corridors and shipping routes were established. They provided the country's initial capital investment and nourished the development of industries.

In the early 2000s, migration patterns changed once again as people began to seek either permanent residence (repatriation) or contractual employment (migrant workers) in Russia. This instigated more flexible types of mobility, including dual citizenship. At the same time, poorly managed practices of temporary labor migration resulted in instances of human trafficking and even slavery. In the minds of Russia's state apparatchiks, including Putin, regulation

[5] *Propiska* verified one's place of residence, approved by the Ministry of the Interior. 'A passport without propiska was considered invalid. A person could live, work, study, vote, send children to school or pre-school, and have access to the social welfare system only in accordance with his/her propiska' (Ivakhnyuk, 2009:5).

of these different patterns of migration was a matter of national security, so new legislation was introduced.

Although crossing borders within the Commonwealth of Independent States (CIS) did not require special visas, in 2003, the Russian government consolidated regulatory measures towards migrants, including quotas on work and temporary visas. These measures were contrary to Russia's economic and demographic interests and also proved counterproductive. Because of inconsistencies and inherent hurdles in obtaining citizenship, the measures served as a deterrent for migration to Russia and fostered infringement, human trafficking, and illegal migration.

In addition, the measures increased tensions not only between the Russian Federation and newly formed neighbouring countries, but also between ethnic Russians and racialized migrants living within the Russian Federation. Putin subsequently made the issue of internal and illegal migration part of his 2012 election campaign, underscoring the importance of increasing the effectiveness of law enforcement and migration services.

In June 2012, the Russian government released the Executive Order on State Migration Policy, which called for further legal action to regulate migration to and from Russia, introducing prison sentences of two to five years for illegally crossing Russia's state borders and up to ten years for illegally crossing the border 'under aggravating circumstances' (Obertyaeva, 2012). Nonetheless, the influx of racialized migrants from the former Soviet republics to Russia, among whom 82 per cent were Muslim, prompted a surge in xenophobia, racism, and nationalism among ethnic Russians, allowing the state to further mobilize its nationalistic rhetoric (Obertyaeva & Stecenko, 2014).

By 2012, when Putin returned to power as Russia's president, the legal mechanisms and practices required to help migrants find employment in Russia had barely been implemented: 'Out of 8.6 million migrants who arrived in Russia after the collapse of the USSR, only 1.6 million received official status and only 500,000 of them received assistance from the state' (Obertyaeva, 2012). Moreover, migration policies were mostly mobilized through unjustified law enforcement practices and 'migrants from Central Asian countries, primarily from Uzbekistan and Tajikistan, occup[ied] the least privileged position in the Russian labour market' (Simon & Sklez, 2023:341). The absence of proper migration policies contributed to the growth of illegal migration and, illegal employment, and their associated problems. Politically, it also aided in fuelling top-down nationalism and shaking nationalist discourse from the bottom-up.

Because of their marginalized status, migrant workers were rarely interested in or given the opportunity to learn Russian and become familiar with the customs of the country. Certain public behaviours of racialized migrants in predominantly ethnic Russian cities – 'for example, celebratory gunfire in the centre of Moscow during a wedding, or lezginka in the subway' – created tension and conflict (Obertyaeva & Stecenko, 2014). Rapid changes in the ethnic composition of Russian society, which is slow in adapting to new norms, consequently generated instances of 'spontaneous nationalism' (Obertyaeva & Stecenko 2014).

The TV show *Nasha Russia/Our Russia* (2006–11) is one example of the state-sponsored performance of spontaneous nationalism, if not outright chauvinism. Mainstream Russian entertainment rarely turns its attention to issues of illegal or labour migration. When it does so, its portrayal of the figure of the migrant ranges from the comic and problematic to the inaccurate and disrespectful. The TV show *Our Russia* was created by an Armenian-born stand-up comedian, Misha Galustyan, who used racial and class stereotypes to tell comic stories from the life of racialized labour migrants and to make fun of Putin's bourgeoisie.

Despite Galustyan's public protestations about his critical use of racial stereotypes to reveal the true face of xenophobia in Russia today, his show was precisely comprised of a set of racial stereotypes employed to gain personal cultural capital and financial profit and to help the state, if not on purpose, to further marshal mechanisms of racial discrimination. In what remains of this section, I turn my attention to theatre works that use the figure of internal migrant to question and resist the homogenizing narratives of nationalist politics, the stereotypes as mobilized by the likes of artists as Galustyan, and policies as manifested by the state.

Following the doctrine of proletarian internationalism, formulated by Marxist philosophy as a brotherhood of all workers whose collective task was to erase borders between nations, Soviet theatre and film widely supported and popularized the narrative of the Friendship of the Peoples, which was reiterated in the 1977 Soviet constitution as one of its foundational values. After the USSR collapsed, the phrase disappeared from common usage and from the language of propaganda, while politically engaged theatre artists and companies sought opportunities to bring the figure of the other, including the racialized migrant, to the stage. Exposing the slogan 'Friendship of the Peoples' as an ideological fake used to efface the complex and conflictual relationships between the peoples of the Soviet Union became their political objective.

For example, in 2003, Teatr.doc produced Alexander Rodionov's *Voyna moldovan za kartonnuyu korobku/The War of the Moldovans for the Cardboard Box*, which was based on a criminal incident perpetrated against migrants from Moldova in one of the Moscow markets. Nine years later, Teatr.doc staged the documentary play *Uzbek* (2012), written and performed by Talgat Batalov, who had migrated from Tashkent. *Uzbek* told the story of an Uzbek migrant in Russia, 'who must pass through a Kafkaesque bureaucracy, in which one's legal documents (such as passport, registration at the place of residence, and work permit) play the most significant role as a marker of one's identity' (Simon & Sklez, 2023:341).

Continuing in this vein, Vsevolod Lisovsky's *Akyn Opera* (2012), also produced by Teatr.doc, not only featured stories of economic migrants but was created by professional migrant actors who used traditional Pamirian songs to enhance their portrayal of experiences of migration to Russia. Since the mid-2010s, Russian theatre has witnessed an increase in productions featuring migrant characters and productions created by migrants, as the wider artistic community began to demonstrate more sensitivity to racialized migrants. Mark Simon and Varavara Sklez observe how some cultural institutions

> refashioned their policies and practices with regards to accessibility for foreigners, multilingualism, and relationships with employees of Central Asian origin in a bid to be more inclusive, though determining how they could successfully reach out to migrant audiences remained a challenge. At the same time, migrants (especially the younger generation who had come from big cities) became more involved in the entertainment sphere (particularly in stand-up comedy). (Simon & Sklez, 2023: 342)

Among productions featuring migrants and experimenting with theatrical forms are Ekaterina Troepol'skaya and Andrey Rodionov's verse play *Svan* (2015), Sergey Davydov's *Respublika/Republic* (2020), and Anastasia Patlay and Nana Grinstein's documentary project *Ne Standart/Non-standard* (2020) stand out. However, Olzhas Zhanaidarov is often cited as the first post-Soviet Russian playwright to address this subject matter. Written in Russian, Zhanaidarov's plays pay special attention to marginalized and racialized migrant characters. Often a person of divided cultural, linguistic, and national loyalties, Zhanaidarov's racialized migrant typically fights for their proper place in contested history of the Soviet Union. At the same time, the migrant remains a victim of the injustices produced by Russia's legislative systems and the diasporic networks to which they belong. By bringing the figure of the racialized migrant into the spotlight, Zhanaidarov seeks acknowledgement of the detrimental impact Russia's corrupt systems of governance have had and continue to have on its non-Russian citizens, both historically and today.

Introducing Zhanaidarov to her readership, the Kazakh journalist Julia Milenkaya emphasizes the artist's complex identity, and the history of his family, which is full of internal migrations and cultural displacements (Milenkaya, 2017). This history inevitably influences Zhanaidarov's theatrical language. 'Born into a Kazakh military family, Zhanaidarov moved to Moscow from Alma-Ata at the age of seven. Since then, he has been living in Moscow, now thinking within the frameworks of the Russian culture' (Milenkaya, 2017). Nevertheless, as a playwright, Zhanaidarov has 'achieved great success in the Russian capital' and 'the plays that brought him this success tell the stories of the Kazakh people' (Milenkaya, 2017).

The winner of many prestigious theatre and literary awards, including the Golden Mask, Zhanaidarov became the artistic director of the Kazakhstan contemporary drama festival, Drama.KZ, in 2017. It took him quite some time to recognize his calling. After studying at the Plekhanov School in Moscow and a short career in business, he began writing literary prose, but it was theatre that brought him moral satisfaction. Writing plays became a therapeutic tool to enable Zhanaidarov to reconcile his identity as a Kazakh child who grew up in Moscow, a Russian writer, and a colonial subject seeking to give voice to non-Russian citizens in Putin's Russia.

Being visibly different and knowing that the colour of one's skin and the shape of one's eyes make one a lesser citizen is the everyday experience of the racialized migrants. Sara Ahmed theorizes this phenomenon as 'stranger-danger' (Ahmed, 2000:24). Zhanaidarov echoes this concept when he recollects his own childhood experiences as a Kazakh boy in Moscow of the mid-1980s, when his classmates and friends, 'as children would often do', reminded him 'with malicious enjoyment' of his racial difference (Zhanaidarov, 2019). This issue would arise with every disagreement, argument, or fight. At that time, Zhanaidarov would 'curse his difference, dreaming of another body, the most ordinary, as long as it looked Slavic' (Zhanaidarov, 2019). Like any teenager, he wanted to belong, to blend with the group, but he knew that his appearance made other children suspicious and wary. He was expected to prove his right to 'a place in the pack', and he did so through his studies, his achievements in sports, and his communication skills.

With time things changed. 'As I grew older, I suddenly discovered the special benefits of my race,' Zhanaidarov writes. 'Childhood with its xenophobic modus vivendi was gone, and I entered the time of my youth and found myself in a university environment, where people were attracted to everything different' (Zhanaidarov, 2019). In certain circles, consumer multiculturalism – from sushi to yoga classes – has grown in, so to be other, to be different, became rewarding. 'When it was to my advantage', he reflects, 'I was a Kazakh; when it was not, I was a Russian' (2019). In the newly forming culture of post-Soviet Russia, to be a visible minority remained problematic, however, specifically as far-right nationalistic and pro-fascist groups were gaining ground. After being beaten up by a group of skinheads on a subway, Zhanaidarov had to admit once again that he would remain forever different, forever other, in Putin's xenophobic Russia (2019).

Zhanaidarov's debut play, *Dzhut* (2013), evidenced both his heightened awareness of being other and also his 'moral obligation to his family and his nation' (Mikova, 2022). Based on the historical events of the Kazakh famine and more specifically on the story of his own grandfather, the play unfolds along two historical timelines. The first plot line plays out in contemporary Moscow and features Yerbol, the grandson of the victims of this famine, and the journalist Elena, an ethnic Russian from the capital. The second plot line takes place in 1930s Kazakhstan, when Akhmet (Yerbol's ancestor) suffers a tragedy when his first wife, Saule, and two young children died of hunger during the Great Famine, despite his cutting off his own fingers to feed his family. *Dzhut* works to remind audiences that the tragedy of forced famine was a fate shared by many ethnic groups in the former Soviet Union. Most had no knowledge of the Kazakhstan famine, and for many Russian speaking readers, *Dzhut* became revelatory and educational.

The word *dzhut* can be translated as 'death of livestock', which often takes place during the long and windy winters of Kazakhstan. A natural phenomenon, *dzhut* holds a special terror for all nomadic peoples, but the *dzhut*, which Zhanaidarov's grandfather survived in his youth, was a man-made disaster organized by the Soviet authorities. Natalia Mikova recalls how 'all property of nomadic and semi-nomadic families was forcefully transported to the settlements under Bolsheviks' control and 'grasslands were stomped to the ground', meaning huge, 'confiscated herds were impossible to feed', so the Kazakh people 'died of starvation or fled' (Mikova, 2022). Only half of the Kazakh population survived the great *dzhut*. For years, however, Kazakh authorities and artists avoided discussing the famine. This was partly because the truth contradicted the accepted Soviet narrative and partly because for Kazakh people, it is ethically unacceptable to speak out about trauma. *Dzhut* became their internalized shame.

Zhanaidarov explains this phenomenon in terms of a particular 'Eastern mentality: Turkic peoples are non-conflictual, and they do not like to air their problems in public, as it seems shameful to them' (in Mikova, 2022). As a writer of mixed cultural upbringing who finds it difficult to support either the patriarchal order of the East or the colonizing practices of the West, Zhanaidarov had to 'break through the traditional Kazakh shame – "uyat" – and bring to the surface the hidden truth of his peoples' history', which was not generally talked about in public (Mikova, 2022).

The play *Dzhut* not only reveals the truth about the Soviet past, but it also highlights unresolvable issues in the Soviet affirmative action policy, which was expected to be beneficial to all ethnic groups residing within the borders of the Soviet Union. It also demonstrates that these unresolved issues are not in the past but continue to produce negative impacts on Kazakhs and other racialized migrants in today's Russia. Writing plays about the suffering of Kazakhs in the official language of the state (Russian) but from embodied experience as a racialized other, Zhanaidarov not only addresses hidden historical injustices but also brings issues of interracial and intercultural relationships, systemic racism, and oppression into the theatrical present and to a wide audience. As a person of multiple cultural loyalties and traditions, Zhanaidarov is able to examine these controversies from a Russian perspective and at the same time from the position of a Kazakh. He is among a very small group of Russian playwrights able to 'study the outcomes of the clashes between Eastern and Russian cultures' (Mikova, 2022). In his 2015 play *Magazine/Store*, Zhanaidarov reveals how historical structures of oppression, corruption, and the abuse of women are reproduced both by migrants and by the Russian authorities, specifically where these structures are mobilized by the host culture.

Store was inspired by events that took place in one of Moscow's grocery stores. For ten years, the owners, migrants themselves, kept a group of young women in slavery. In a distressingly familiar story, the victims were brought to Moscow for work but never received wages and had their passports confiscated. They gave the young women nicknames, shaved their heads, repeatedly abused and raped them, and sold their newborn babies for organs. Zhanaidarov based his play on police records related to this crime and on documents collected by the human rights activists who set the girls free. He wrote *Store* to make visible the psychological and legal mechanisms of modern-day slavery.

A type of modern tragedy, *Store* examines the origins of everyday and systemic racism and totalitarianism, in which 'the semblance of justice is accomplished by making a new crime' (Banasukevich, 2016). Structured around a dramatic juxtaposition between two female characters, Ziyash, the store's owner, and Karlygash, her slave, the play describes the inhumane conditions of labour that many racialized migrants are subjected to in Russia. Yet both women are also victims of their home culture's patriarchy, in which women are often little more than the domestic slaves of their fathers or husbands.

After being repeatedly abused by her husband, Ziyash relocates to Moscow. Here, she is determined to survive and believes she can do this only by enslaving other women. For her business to thrive, Ziyash needs special protection, so she strikes a pact with local police officers, who function as her proprietors and guards. By revealing the multiple layers of corruption and abuse that many racialized migrants fall victim to, Zhanaidarov obviously condemns systemic racism and oppression. He also speaks to issues of patriarchy as deeply engrained within Kazakh traditional culture, and to the problems of illegal migration, exploitation, and violence as practised by Russian authorities, members of law enforcement, and individuals.

In *Store*, what begins as a kind of 'social drama from the life of the urban poor, gradually acquires metaphysical features' as the 'brutality of the women's life turns into a horror show' (Fedyanina, 2018). Zhanaidarov reaches for the vocabulary of magic realism. At the play's resolution, Ziyash is brutally murdered by skinheads who also vandalize her store. These horrible events are a magical projection of Karlygash's desire for salvation and revenge. In reality, there were no skinheads/saviours to 'resolve' the situation. A relative of one of the slaves pleaded the girl's cause with human rights activists (Banasukevich, 2016).

In an effort to explain his choice of topic, Zhanaidarov compares the position of racialized migrants in Russia to other examples of human slavery produced by different totalitarian regimes: 'slavery, that is, the power of one man over another, has always been there. Our history demonstrates that people do not change, nor do their methods of violence', they are always 'based on the erasure of an individual' (Zhanaidarov in Kataeva, 2018). Zhanaidarov nevertheless remains acutely sensitive to the fact that his characters are racialized migrants: 'Karlygash came to Moscow from Kazakhstan to earn money for her house. Once in the store, she undergoes all the humiliation and suffering a person can endure, and at some point, she feels like a sacrificial lamb' (Zhanaidarov in Kataeva, 2018).

In the eyes of Ziyash and those ethnic Russians who collaborate in her crimes, Karlygash remains a second-class citizen. To audiences in Moscow, the issue of illegal migration remains barely visible, although, as Zhanaidarov notes, it has become impossible to pretend that racialized migrants and native Russians live in Moscow separate from each other. He argues that to improve the situation, migrant labour must be legalized and protected (Kataeva 2018). Writing plays like *Store* can not only help bring the figure of the migrant into the theatrical spotlight, but it can also make Russian legislative organs and institutions regulating migration recognize racialized migrants as human subjects, not just faceless numbers in bureaucratic cases.

Like *Dzhut*, however, the first production of *Store* did not take place in Moscow, but in Tatarstan at the Almetyevsk Tatar Theatre. The earlier play was first produced in the city of Ufa, the capital of Bashkortostan, which is the fourth-most populous city in the Volga Federal District. *Dzhut* was directed by Ajrat Abushakhmanov, the artistic director of the M. Gafuriri Bashkir Drama Theatre. The theme of collective hunger instigated by the Soviet authorities was close to the people of Bashkortostan, who also suffered forced famine.

To make the story of *Dzhut* speak directly to Bashkir people, Abushakhmanov translated the historical Kazakh part of the play into the Bashkir language, while keeping the contemporary part, which takes place in Moscow, in Russian. Later, the play was staged in Kazakhstan, in Russian, in Lermontov State Drama Theatre in Almaty, with the audience being very receptive and appreciative that this forbidden topic was finally brought to the stage. When Zhanaidarov translated *Dzhut* into the Kazakh language, it was staged by other Kazakh companies too.

In 2018, the Almetyevsk Tatar Theatre invited Eduard Shakhov to direct Zhanaidarov's *Store* in Tatar. Explaining his vision for the production, Shakhov emphasized its humanitarian message – the need to recognize violence as the 'collapse of the individual, degradation of people [and] loss of humanity' (Kosyakova 2018). For Shakhov, *Store* gave voice to a specific type of violence, one rooted in traditional culture and at the same time encouraged by the state. It focused on the conflict between two women as a metaphorical reflection of power structures in the society in which they live, with Ziyash standing in for the authorities and Karlygash representing rightless people who can be easily abused. To Shakhov, this conflict creates the atmosphere and the conditions of total unfreedom, which he chose to depict on stage through the choreography of two female bodies, in words and in movement.

When the Almetyevsk Tatar Theatre brought its production to Moscow as part of the 2018 Golden Mask Theatre Festival, *Store* was performed on the stage of Teatr Naciy/Theatre of Nations, which aims 'to establish an international theatre dialogue and bring the creative energy of international theatre to its stage' (Teatr Naciy). Shakhov's staging of *Store* received many positive reviews, although some of them exhibited a deeply familiar attitude of superiority and snobbery to the racialized subjects of Russia. For example, the influential Moscow theatre critic Olga Fedyanina wrote:

> *Store* turned out to be a production to which the definition 'provincial' – in its traditional sense – does not apply. It exhibits such unrestrained, unprovincial sharpness and certainty of social and artistic statements . . . The fact that the Moscow audience received the play with the same interest as the home audience in Almetyevsk is a great accomplishment of the theatre itself. (Fedyanina, 2018)

This quote reveals how deeply colonial attitudes are ingrained in the Russian psyche: the reviewer speaks from her position in the centre of the empire, although she remains an educated person of liberal views and writes from good intentions. This chauvinism continues to mark the everyday experiences of racialized migrants in Russia, not only because it permits everyday racism in Russia, but also because it permeates migration laws themselves. *Store* describes precisely this situation of injustice and demonstrates how interracial humiliation and abuse is deeply rooted in the psyche of many Russian citizens, both minority and majority ethnic. The critic Natalia Mikova notes that Zhanaidarov often 'compares Kazakh traditional culture and post-Soviet culture' asking how far 'such a comparison jeopardize[s] the relationship between the metropolis and the former colonies, nurturing the bitter fruits of the un-neighbourliness that we are witnessing in Ukraine' (Mikova, 2022). Zhanaidarov insists that all ethnic groups from the Soviet empire share the trauma of the colonial past, and thus share the responsibility to reflect critically on it. By staging plays about Soviet Kazakhstan or non-ethnic Russians in Russia today, contemporary Russian theatre can emphasize the urgency of this topic. Moreover, it can 'expose the conflict of Eastern and Western civilizations, focusing on migration as the process of interpenetration of cultures' (Milenkaya, 2017).

Conclusion: From Nationalism to Totalitarianism

On 31 December 2022, Putin gave his traditional New Year's address. Unlike in previous years, however, the video featured neither the illuminated proverbial Spasskaya Tower nor a Christmas tree. Instead, Putin appeared with a group of Russian paratroopers in fatigues in the background, standing shoulder to shoulder, ready to fight for their country and president. The video was filmed almost a year after Russia's full-scale invasion of Ukraine in which thousands of Ukrainians perished and millions sought refuge outside their own country. Ukraine's infrastructure and economy had been severely damaged. Thousands of Russian soldiers had been killed at the front and the international community had imposed heavy economic sanctions, turning the country into a pariah state. Yet Putin's address ignored this reality. Instead, it rehashed the quintessential rhetoric and ideological and moral foundations of new nationalism in Russia, which by now had transformed into a resurgent totalitarianism. In this sense, the speech reflected the escalation of control and suppression the Russian state has implemented against its own people since the invasion of Ukraine.

The witch hunt began apace in March 2022, when most of the independent media was shut down, including the *Echo Moskvy* radio station, the *Rain* TV channel, the *Novaya Gazeta* newspaper – whose editor-in-chief Dmitry Muratov was the recipient of the 2021 Nobel Peace Prize – and quite strikingly in relation to the content of this Element, the oldest Russian theatre journal *Teatr*. Many theatre directors were fired, theatre companies – including Serebrennikov's Gogol Centre – were shut down, and critically engaged artists fled the country.

This ominous atmosphere of fear and intolerance intensified in the summer, with the State Duma passing new amendments to the previously implemented Foreign Agents Law (The State Duma, 2022b), which made individuals, not organizations, accountable for their actions, statements, and sources of income.[6] On 9 November 2022, Putin signed the Decree N 809 on traditional values (The State Duma, 2022c), and on 24 November 2022, the State Duma passed the anti-LGBTQ

[6] This law came to effect on 1 December 2022.

propaganda law (The State Duma, 2022d). The objective was to instill collective fear and the expectation of worse to come, and thus to 'divert Russian citizens' attention from the war in Ukraine' and 'to impose an image of an external enemy, so that they forget that the real enemies are those who usurped power in the country and are now desperately trying to hold on to it' (FEM, 2022).

This hastily introduced legislation produced an immediate impact on the work of all cultural institutions, with another wave of Russian artists fleeing into exile, performances being closed, the names of directors and choreographers taken off posters and programs, and individual artists dismissed from their positions. Conversely, it has also resulted in many artists openly cooperating with the investigative committee and creating new partnerships with theatre companies in the occupied territories, such as the collaboration between the Mariupol State Theatre, whose building was shelled to rubble by Russian forces, and Moscow's Theatre of Nations. Individual artists have organized concerts in Donbass, and patriotically minded poets and writers have composed poems and plays to glorify the Russian army fighting in Ukraine, while the state-sponsored TV channels and patriotically minded influencers have escalated the production of propaganda. For example, on the eve of the first anniversary of the invasion, the popular singer Vika Tsyganova released a new single 'Mama Rossia/Mother Russia', which was her third song in a patriotic cycle glorifying the military might of the private mercenary Wagner Group and its founder Evgeny Prigozhin (Nakhimov, 2023). Riddled with conspiracy references and images, the lyrics of the song openly called for a Russian nuclear attack and utilized images of monsters and reptiles to represent the collective West in a fight with the proverbial Russian bear. Musically, the arrangement quoted from Richard Wagner's compositions, which cemented the song's connection to the Nazis, who famously appropriated Wagner's music.

This wide range of artistic responses to the invasion of Ukraine reflects a deep polarization in Russian society as artists have now been forced to produce art against a backdrop of powerful propaganda and punitive legislation and in a climate of conformism, fear, depression, and complacency. The position of artists with a clear anti-war stance has become particularly dangerous. On 5 May 2023, the Moscow-based theatre director Evgenia (Zhenya) Berkovich and the playwright Svetlana Petriichuk were detained as witnesses and charged with terrorism under Article 205.2 of the Criminal Code of the Russian Federation, 'Public calls to terrorist activity, public justification of terrorism or propaganda of terrorism', which potentially carries a seven-year sentence (Criminal Code, 1996:176). Their production *Finist the Brave Falcon* (2020), produced by Berkovich's theatre company, SOSO Daughters, and a recipient of national Golden Mask awards for Best Work of a Costume Designer and Best Work of a Playwright, was cited as evidence. This accusation has effectively made the Berkovich/Petriichuk case the first criminal case in Putin's Russia, in which the artists are to be tried for their artistic expression. Like many of the artists discussed in this Element, personal history has shaped both the form and content of these artists' work. Yet Berkovich's position stands out as her theatre is deeply rooted in her personal experience 'of rejection as a minority subject' – that is, as a woman and as a Jew (Berkovich in Polikhovich, 2020).

Born into a Jewish-Soviet family, Berkovich remains highly sensitive to issues of survival, gender discrimination, and racism. She expresses her self-awareness as a minoritarian subject – a Jew, a woman, a theatre director, a poet, and a mother of two adopted children – in a specific linguistic and political demand. She insists on using the feminine ending 'ka' in all nouns that refer to the everyday or professional activities of women. For example, she demands that the word 'director' – *rezhisser* in Russian – be written and pronounced as '*rezhisserka*'/'*directorka*', to indicate her gender positionality as a theatre maker. This practice is revolutionary because in the Russian language, many nouns used to designate professions are masculine and take the ending 'or' or 'er'. For Berkovich, challenging this linguistic practice is the first step on the road to demanding respect and recognition for women working in theatre, and society more generally.

A graduate of the St. Petersburg Academy of Theatre Arts class of 2007, Berkovich studied directing with Kirill Serebrennikov at the Moscow Art Theatre School. Her graduation piece was a production of Jean Anouilh's *The Lark* (2012) produced at the Moscow Art Theatre's New Stage. Written in 1952, Anouilh's play concerns the trial, conviction, and execution of Joan of Arc. Berkovich's production turned it into a metaphor for the Russian justice system that is at once broken and discriminatory. Joan of Arc, the protagonist of Anouilh's play, is a fierce female teenager forced to face systemic violence and discrimination, key themes in Berkovich's later work.

After graduating, Berkovich worked in many state-funded theatres but soon realized she did not want any part of the systemic violence that flourished in these institutions. Stagnation, nepotism, backstabbing, aggression towards women, and artistic inertia pushed Berkovich towards the independent theatre scene, which privileged collegiality, dispersed leadership, and inclusivity in arts management. Berkovich embraced these practices, not least because she preferred to control her own work independent of the restrictive repertoire plans of state-funded institutions. In 2018, she created an independent theatre collective, SOSO Daughters, whose objective was to give voice to women and to advocate for an 'the ethics of care' as a feminist strategy of artistic survival under the pressure of Putin's regime (Nikolaeva, 2022:95).

Finist the Brave Falcon, a cause of Berkovich and Petriichuk's arrest and accusations of the calls for terrorism, tells the story of a group of young Russian women groomed by Islamic terrorists on social media. These women leave their homes in search of love but find only abuse and betrayal at the hands of their new husbands, who happened to be ISIS fighters. Disappointed in their marriages, they decide to return home. Upon arrival in Russia, however, they are arrested, put on trial, and imprisoned. The dialogue of *Finist the Brave Falcon* draws on interviews with the victims and court proceedings, but it uses a traditional Russian fairy tale as its framing device, so the play infuses the action with metaphor and allegory.

Strong anti-terrorist work, *Finist the Brave Falcon* presents its female characters as victims of skillful seducers. They are reminiscent of a resourceful village girl, Mar'yushka, the protagonist of the Russian fairy tale that gave Petriichuk's play its name, who is searching for her beloved. In the fairy tale, Mar'yushka outsmarts a queen, breaks a spell, and is rewarded with a happy ending. In *Finist the Brave Falcon*, each young woman turns into a new Mar'yushka to relate her own version of the tale and to realize that her own story will have no happy ending.

The action moves from one horrific episode to another and in so doing forces the audience to question why, in a country that has declared the traditional family the basis of its nation-building project, women seek love, understanding, and respect elsewhere, even to the extent of being susceptible to grooming by a terrorist organization. The production portrays these women as casualties of the ongoing violence of the nationalist project, but also suggests that if (in real life) violence breeds violence, in theatre, at least an alternative might be found. By centring female experience, *Finist the Brave Falcon* brings empathy back to the stage. This call to empathy has been a consistent theme in much of the work discussed in this Element. It has been used variously as a strategy to undermine, problematize, challenge, and complicate the worst simplifications and excesses of Putin's nationalist project.

I bring this short study of political resistance in contemporary Russian theatre and the performative nature of Russian nationalism to a close with a brief observation. Nationalism is a powerful and dangerous sociopolitical construct. Historically, it has helped mobilize the work of modernization in certain cultural contexts, but it has also been intrinsic to the development of deadly political variants such as totalitarianism and fascism. The theatre and performance projects explored in this Element are illustrative of how nationalism can be both promoted and resisted through the arts.

I have also sought to demonstrate the extent to which the Russian authorities are prepared to control and censor, if not crush, any artistic expression that questions the homogenizing discourses of nationalism. For now, mass terror is a weapon of control and distraction that Putin's government employs selectively and performatively against its own people, mostly for propaganda purposes. As history teaches us, however, in Russia, life tends to imitate art, and it may not be too long before Putin's performance of power transforms fully into wholesale aggression and oppression of the people.

References

Ahmed, Sara. (2000). *Strange Encounters: Embodied Others in Post-coloniality*. London: Routledge.

Anderson, Benedict. (1991). *Imagined Communities: Reflections on the Origin and Spread of Nationalism*. London: Verso.

Arendt, Hannah. (1962). *The Origins of Totalitarianism*. Cleveland, OH: Meridian.

Arutyunova, Ekaterina & Konstantin Zamyatin. (2021). An Ethnolinguistic Conflict on the Compulsory Learning of the State Languages in the Republics of Russia: Policies and Discourses. *International Journal of Human Rights*, 25:5, pp. 832–52.

Autant-Mathieu, Marie-Christine. (2020). The Story of Russian-Language Drama since 2000 PostDoc, the Postdramatic and Teatr Post. In Curtis, Julie A. E., ed., *New Drama in Russian: Performance, Politics and Protest in Russia, Ukraine and Belarus*. London: Bloomsbury, pp. 23–40.

Banasukevich, Anna. (2016). Rabovladenie XXI veka [Slave-Owning in the 21st Century]. *Peterburskiy Teatral'niy Zhurnal*. 9 November. https://ptj.spb.ru/blog/rabovladenie-xxiveka.

Behrens, Wolfang. (2021). Wanted: Nose. Interview with Kirill Serebrennikov. *Bayerische Staatsoper*. www.staatsoper.de/inhalte-home/editorial-die-nase.

Benjamin, Walter. (2003). On the Concept of History. In Eiland, Howard, and Jennings, Michael W., eds., *Selected Writings: Volume 4 (1938–1940)*. Cambridge, MA: Belknap Press of Harvard University Press, pp. 388–400.

Beumers, Birgit & Mark Lipovetsky. (2009). *Performing Violence: Literary and Theatrical Experiments of New Russian Drama*. London: Intellect.

Bhabha, Homi. (1990). *On Nation and Narration*. New York: Routledge.

Billig, Michael. (2010). *Banal Nationalism*. London: SAGE.

Boutsko, Anastassia. (2020). Kirill Serebrennikov: Prison Sentence Looms for Celebrated Russian Director. *Deutsche Welle (DW)*. 25 June. www.dw.com/en/kirill-serebrennikov-prison-sentence-looms-for-celebrated-russian-director/a-53938876.

Bull, John. (2018). Introduction. *Journal of Contemporary Drama in English*, 6:1, pp. 1–14.

Burrett, Tina. (2020). Evaluating Putin's Propaganda Performance 2000–2018: Stagecraft As Statecraft. In Snow, Nancy, Baines, Paul, and

O'Shaughnessy, Nicholas, eds., *The SAGE Handbook of Propaganda*. London: SAGE, pp. 492–509.

Butler, Judith. (2015). *Notes toward a Performative Theory of Assembly*. Cambridge, MA: Harvard University Press.

Constitution of the Russian Federation. (2020). https://rm.coe.int/constitution-of-the-russian-federation-en/1680a1a237.

Council Implementing Regulation (EU) 2022/1270 of 21July2022. https://eur-lex.europa.eu/legal-content/EN/TXT/?uri=celex%3A32022R1270.

Criminal Code of the Russian Federation. (1996). N 63-FZ, as amended on 29 December 2022. Revision effective from 1 January 2023. 6 June. https://snab28.ru/upload/iblock/43d/fcxco48uwkxufcejqgpaviu5vvhcibc1/uk.pdf.

Curtis, Julie A. E. (2020). *New Drama in Russian: Performance, Politics and Protest in Russia, Ukraine and Belarus*. London: Bloomsbury Academic, pp. 1–22.

Davydova, Marina. (2007). Deti na scene igrali v gestapo [Children Played Gestapt on Stage]. *Izvestiya*. 5 May. https://mxat.ru/history/performance/man-pillow/10067.

(2018). The Putin Show: Kirill Serebrennikov and Russia's Conservative Revolution. *Eurozone*. 9 February. www.eurozine.com/putin-show-kirill-serebrennikov-russias-conservative-revolution.

De la Torre, Lucia. (2021). Balabanov's Ganster Film *Brat* Shook, Explained and Defined 90s Russia. *Calvert Journal*. 26 August. www.calvertjournal.com/articles/show/13062/film-of-the-week-brother-balabanov-mubi-russia-90s-arthouse-gangster-st-petersburg.

Dugin, Aleksandr. (1997). Fascism: Borderless and Red. Trans. by Umland, Andreas. https://historynewsnetwork.org/article/88134.

(2000). *Osnovy geopolitiki. Geopoliticheskoe buduschee Rossii. Myslit' Prostranstvom [The Foundations of Geopolitics: The Geopolitical Future of Russia]*. Moscow: Arktogeya-tsentr.

(2022). Nachinaetsya: glavnaya stat'ya Alexandra Dugina [It Is about to Begin: Major Article by Alezander Dugin]. *Tsar.Grad*. 15 September. https://tsargrad.tv/articles/nachinaetsja-glavnaja-statja-aleksandra-dugina_625556.

Egorov, Oleg. (2018). 'Children's Friend': The Dark Story behind Stalin's Popular Photo with a Soviet Girl. *Russia Beyond*. 15 June. www.rbth.com/history/328538-stalin-children-gelya-markizova.

Emel'yanenko, Vladimir. (2016). V Gogol'-Centre 'Pokhorony Stalina' sobrali anshlag [At the Gogol Centre *Stalin's Funeral* Is Sold Out]. *Rossijskaya gazeta*. 16 December. https://rg.ru/2016/12/26/v-gogol-centre-pohorony-stalina-sobrali-anshlag.html.

Etkind, Alexander. (2011). *Internal Colonization: Russia's Imperial Experience*. Cambridge: Polity Press.

Fatykhova, Nuria. (2020a). Mne stalo interesno, a kto takie tatary dlja samih sebja [I Was Wondering Who Tatars Are for Themselves] *Business Online*. 21 November. www.business-gazeta.ru/article/489272.

(2020b). Zulejha protiv Zulejhi [Zulejha against Zulejhi]. *Colta*. 8 May. www.colta.ru/articles/art/24311-spory-o-zuleyhe-i-sovetskiy-imperializm.

Fedyanina, Olga. (2018). Zhizn' na scene [Life on Stage]. *Kommersant*. 24 March. www.kommersant.ru/doc/3584131.

FEM. (2022). Redakciya 'LGBT – Propagandy' o zaprete LGBT – propagandy [Editorial 'LGBT – Propaganda' on Prohibition of LGBT – Propaganda]. Telegram Channel: Feministskoe Antivoennoe Soprotivelnie. 24 November. https://t.me/femagainstwar/6148.

Freedman, John. (2020). Teatr.doc and the Struggle for Authenticity and Relevance in Contemporary

Russian Drama and Theatre. In Warner, Vessela S. & Manole, Diana, eds., *Staging Postcommunism: Alternative Theatre in Eastern and Central Europe after 1989*. Iowa City: University of Iowa Press, pp. 76–90.

Freud, Sigmund. (1949). *Group Psychology and the Analysis of the Ego*. London: Hogarth Press and the Institute of Psycho-analysis.

Fry, Tony & Madina Tlostanova. (2021). *A New Political Imagination: Making the Case*. Abingdon: Routledge.

Gessen, Masha. (2022). 'Z' Is the Symbol of the New Russian Politics of Aggression. *New Yorker*. 22 March. www.newyorker.com/news/our-columnists/z-is-the-symbol-of-the-new-russian-politics-of-aggression.

Goncharov, Vladislav. (2020). Zulejha – eto recidiv amerikanskoy propagandy [Zulejha Is a Relapse of American Propaganda]. *Komsomol'skaya Pravda*. 16 April. https://radiokp.ru/zuleykha-eto-recidiv-amerikanskoy-propagandy-suraykin-o-seriale-i-vragakh-naroda_nid18158_au4311au.

Gudkov, Lev. (2015). Putin's Relapse into Totalitarianism. In Lipman, M. & Petrov, N., eds., *The State of Russia: What Comes Next?* London: Palgrave Pivot, pp. 86–109.

(2018). Vtorichniy, ili vozvratniy, totalitarism [Secondary or Recurring Totalitarianism]. *Vestnik obschestvennogo mneniya*, 3–4:127, pp. 207–60.

Hanukai, Maksim. (2020). Resurrection by Surrogation: Spectral Performance in Putin's Russia. *Slavic Review*, 79:4, pp. 800–24.

Hobsbawm, Eric J. (1989). *The Age of Empire, 1875–1914*. New York: Vintage.

Holdsworth, Nadine. (2010). *Theatre & Nation*. London: Palgrave Macmillan.

Hummel, Daniel. (2017). Banal Nationalism, National Anthems, and Peace. *Peace Review*, 29:2, pp. 25–30.

Ivakhnyuk, Irina. (2009). Russian Migration Policy and Its Impact on Human Development. *Human Development Research Paper Series*, No. 14. https://mpra.ub.uni-muenchen.de/19196/1/MPRA_paper_19196.pdf.

Jonson, Lena. (2018). Russia: Culture, Cultural Policy, and the Swinging Pendulum of Politics. In Bernsand, Niklas & Törnquist-Plewa, Barbara, eds., *Cultural and Political Imaginaries in Putin's Russia*. Eurasian Studies Library 11. Leiden: Brill: pp. 13–36.

Kaluzhsky, Mikhail. (2015). Pamyat' Doc, *Teatr*, N. 19. https://oteatre.info/pamyat-doc.

Karas', Alena et al. (2019). Krugly stol 'Teatr i istoricheskaya pamyat' [Round Table 'Theatre and Historical Memory']. *St. Petersburgskiy Teatralniy Journal*, 2:96. https://ptj.spb.ru/archive/96/memory-place/kruglyj-stol-teatr-iistoricheskaya-pamyat.

Kataeva, Nina. (2018). Evgeniy Mironov: Mockvichi i peterburzhcy letayut na prem'ery v Ekaterinburg i Perm' [Evgeniy Mironov: Moscowites and St Petersburgers Fly to Ekaterinburg and Perm for Premieres]. *Akrida*. 23 March. www.akrida.ru/articles/16857.html.

Kolyazin, Vladimir. (2022). Gde serp, tam I molot [If There Is a Sickle, There Will Be a Hammer]. *Ekran i Scena*. N. 4. 25 February. https://screenstage.ru/?p=16431.

Kosyakova, Natalia. (2018). Talanty is provincii – Moskve [Provincial Talents Come to Moscow]. *Klauzura*. 23 March. https://klauzura.ru/2018/03/talanty-iz-provintsii-moskve-spektakli-pobediteli-xv-festival-malyh-gorodov-rossii-na-stsene-teatra-natsij.

Koulos, Thanos. (2021). Nationalism and the Lost Homeland: The Case of Greece. *Nations and Nationalism*, 27, pp. 482–96.

Kudors, Andis. (2010). 'Russian World': Russia's Soft Power Approach to Compatriots Policy, *Russian Analytical Digest. Research Centre for East European Studies*. 81:10, pp. 2–4.

Laruelle, Marlene. (2015). Dangerous Liaisons. In Laruelle, Marlene, ed., *Eurasianism and the European Far Right: Reshaping the Europe–Russia Relationship*. London: Lexington Books, pp. 1–32.

(2019). *Russian Nationalism: Imaginaries, Doctrines, and Political Battlefields*. London: Routledge.

Malinova, Olga. (2018). Politika pamyati kak oblast' simvolicheskoy poliitki [The Politics of Memory As a Field of Symbolic Politics]. In Miller, A. I. & Efremenko D. B., eds., *Metodologicheskie voprosy isycheniya politiki pamyati*. Moscow – St. Petersburg: Nestor-Istoriya, pp. 27–54.

(2019). Constructing the 'Usable Past': The Evolution of the Official Historical Narrative in Post-Soviet Russia. In Bernsand, Niklas &

Törnquist Plewa, Barbara, eds., *Cultural and Political Imaginaries in Putin's Russia*. Leiden: Brill, pp. 85–104.

Martin, Terry. (2001). An Affirmative Action Empire: The Soviet Union As the Highest Form of Imperialism Identity and Theories of Empire. In Suny, Ronald Grigor., et al., eds., *A State of Nations Empire and Nation-Making in the Age of Lenin and Stalin*. Oxford: Oxford University Press, pp. 67–90.

Mignolo, Walter & Rolando Vazquez. (2013). Decolonial AestheSis: Colonial Wounds/Decolonial Healings, *social text online*. 15 July. https://socialtextjournal.org/periscope_article/decolonial-aesthesis-colonial-woundsdecolonial-healings.

Mikova, Natalia. (2022). Olzhas-Alzhas: Sceny kazahskogo goloda [Scenes from Hunger in Kazakhstan]. *S-T-O-L*. 28 March. https://s-t-o-l.com/material/26940-olzhas-alzhas-stseny-kazakhskogo-goloda.

Milenkaya, Julia. (2017). Chelovek, kotory otkryl temu kazahskogo dhuta rossiyskoy auditorii [The Man Who Brought the Topic of Kazakh Famine to the Russian Audience]. *Ratel.KZ*. 28 October. https://ratel.kz/outlook/chelovek_kotoryj_otkryl_temu_kazahskogo_dzhuta_rossijskoj_auditorii.

Militz, Elisabeth & Carolin Schurr. (2016). Affective Nationalism: Banalities of Belonging in Azerbaijan, *Political Geography*, 14, pp. 54-63.

Milosevich-Juaristi, Mira. (2018). The Immortal Regiment: The Pride and Prejudice of Russia. Elcano Royal Institute. 27 September. www.realinstitutoelcano.org/en/analyses/the-immortal-regiment-the-pride-and-prejudice-of-russia.

Nakhimov, Sergey. (2023) Vika Tsyganova 'Mama Rossiya': Puvica prodolzhet 'sadirat'; Zapad ['Mother Russia': Singer Continued to 'Challenge' the West]. *AmalNews*. 24 February. https://amalantra.ru/vika-tsyganova-mama-rossiya.

Nikerichev, Andrei. (2020). Serebrennikov Trial: Russia Gives Suspended Sentence to Prominent Director in Fraud Case. *Moscow Times*. 26 June. www.themoscowtimes.com/2020/06/26/serebrennikov-trial-russia-gives-suspended-sentence-to-prominent-director-in-fraud-case-a70708.

Nikolaeva, Olga. (2022). Keep Calm, the Corridor Will Be Open Soon: Soso Daughters, Representation of Trauma and Independent Creative Practice in Contemporary Russian Theatre. *Nordic Theatre Studies*, 33:1, pp. 87–105.

Obertyaeva, Irina. (2012). Migracionnaya politika postsovetskoy Rossii: Transformaciya podhodov k ee formirovaniyu [Migration Policy of Post-Soviet Russia: Transformation of Approaches to Its Formation]. *Vestnik VGTU*, N 12. https://cyberleninka.ru/article/n/migratsionnaya-politika-postsovetskoy-rossii-transformatsiya-podhodov-k-ee-formirovaniyu.

Obertyaeva, Irina & Anatoly Stecenko. (2014). Ethnocentrism i migraciya v poli-etnicheskom rossiyskom obschestve [Ethnocentrism and Migration in a Multi-ethnic Russian Society]. *Vestnik VGTU*. N 10:2, pp. 90–3. https://cyberleninka.ru/article/n/etnotsentrizm-i-migratsiya-v-polietnicheskom-rossiyskom-obschestve/viewer.

Ostrovsky, Arkady. (2016). *The Invention of Russia: From Gorbachev's Freedom to Putin's War*. London: Viking.

Pal'veleva, Lilya. (2022). Tri plasta pamyati. Spektakl o zhertvakh gosudarstvennogo nasiliya [Three Layers of Memory: A Play about Victims of State Violence]. *Radio Svoboda*. 25 February. www.svoboda.org/a/tri-plasta-pamyati-spektaklj-o-zhertvah-gosudarstvennogo-nasiliya/31706642.html.

Pastukhov, Vladimir. (2022). Zagovor chernykh filosofov [Black Philosophers' Conspiracy]. *Novaya Media*. 3 October. https://novaya.media/articles/2022/10/03/zagovor-chernykh-filosofov.

Patlay, Anastasiya & Nana Grinstein. (2020). Document kak otsutstvie. Rabota v teatre s istoricheskoy pamyat'ju [Document As Absence: Working with Historical Memory in Theatre]. *Iskusstvo Kino*. 1:2, pp. 155–64.

(2022). Interview with the Author. 5 August.

Pearson, Raymond. (1989). Privileges, Rights, and Russification. In Crisp O. & L. Edmondson, eds., *Civil Rights in Imperial Russia*. Oxford: Clarendon, pp. 86–102.

Polikhovich, Alexej. (2020). 'Kurica ne ptica, baba ne rezhisser' ['A Hen Is Not a Bird, a Woman Is Not a Director']. *Takie Dela*. 26 October. https://takiedela.ru/2020/11/kurica-ne-ptica-baba-ne-rezhisser.

Rajkina, Marina. (2002). Plastilinnovye ludi. Tree pissyara i odin grob. *MK*. 23 January. www.smotr.ru/pressa/text/rai_plast.htm.

Renan, Ernest. (1990). What Is a Nation? In Bhabha, Homi, ed., *On Nation and Narration*. New York: Routledge. pp. 8–22.

RIA NOVOSTI. (2016). Cerebrennikov rasskazal o 'Pokhoronakh Stalina' v 'Gogol-centre' [Serebrennikov Told Us about Staging 'Stalin's Funeral' at the 'Gogol Centre']. 22 December. https://ria.ru/20161222/1484308302.html.

Robinson, Paul. (2019). *Russian Conservatism*. Ithaca, NY: Cornell University Press.

Rokem, Freddie. (2000). *Performing History: Theatrical Representations of the Past in Contemporary Theatre*. Iowa City: University of Iowa Press.

Rubin, Julia. (1996). Meditations on Russia: Yeltsin Calls for New National 'Idea'. *AP NEWS*. 2 August. https://apnews.com/article/122cd732a8cf8b35989afeec4db69dcd.

Schuler, Catherine. (2015). Priamaia liniia s Vladimirom Putinym: Performing Democracy Putin-Style. *TDR*, 59:1, pp. 136–60.

Sennett, Richard. (2011). *The Foreigner: Two Essays on Exile*. London: Notting Hill Editions.

Senshin, Evgeniy & Lev Gudkov. (2022). 'Vosem' priznakov togo, chto rezhim v Rossii iz avtoritarnogo stal totalitarnym ['Eight' Signs That the Regime in Russia Has Gone from Authoritarian to Totalitarian]. *Republic*. 5 September. https://republic.ru/posts/105098.

Serebrennikov, Kirill. (2009). Foreword. In Beumers, Birgit & Lipovetsky, Mark, eds., *Performing Violence: Literary and Theatrical Experiments of New Russian Drama*. Bristol: Intellect, pp. 9–13.

Shchedrovitsky, Petr. (2000). Russkiy mir i transnacional'noe russkoe [Russian World and Transnational Russian]. *Russkiy Zhurnal*. 2 March. www.russ.ru/politics/meta/20000302_schedr.html.

Shekhovtsov, Anton. (2015). Alexander Dugin and the West European New Right, 1989–1994. In Laruelle, Marlene, ed., *Eurasianism and the European Far Right: Reshaping the Europe–Russia Relationship*. London: Lexington Books, pp. 35–76.

Shenderova, Alla. (2007). Kirill Serebrennikov priglashaet na kazn [Kirill Serebrennikov Invites for Beheading]. *Kommersant*. 12 May. https://mxat.ru/history/performance/man-pillow/10054.

Sila Kultury. (2017). Za chto mir lubit Kirilla Serebrennikova? [Why People in the World Like Kirill Serebrennikov?] *Sila Kul'tury*. 30 May. https://silakultura.ru/article/za-chto-mir-lyubit-kirilla-serebrennikova.

Sitdikov, Ramil. (2022). Mashkov rasskazal, kak bukva Z poyavilas' na zdanii Театра Табакоvа [Mashkov Told How the Letter Z Appeared on the Building of the Tabakov Theatre]. *RIA.Novosti*. 29 March. https://ria.ru/20220329/mashkov-1780739231.html.

Sklez, Varvara. (2019). Voyna i emansipaciya. Kak govorit' o zhenskoy istorii v teatre? [War and Emancipation: How Does Theatre Talk about Women's History?] Moscow: Sakharov Center. 29 May. Unpublished transcript.

Sklez, Varvara & Mark Simon. (2023). Migrant Artists and Precarious Labour in Contemporary Russian Theatre. In Meerzon, Yana & Wilmer, S. E., eds., *Palgrave Handbook on Theatre and Migration*. London: Palgrave Macmillan, pp. 339–52.

Smith, Anthony D. (2001). *Nationalism: Theory, Ideology, History*. New York: Polity Press.

Snyder, Timothy. (2018). Ivan Ilyin, Putin's Philosopher of Russian Fascism. *New York Review*. 16 March. www.nybooks.com/online/2018/03/16/ivan-ilyin-putins-philosopher-of-russian-fascism.

Staliūnas, Darius. *Making Russians: Meaning and Practice of Russification in Lithuania and Belarus after 1863*. Amsterdam: Rodopi, 2007.

State Duma of the Russian Federation. (1995). Federal Constitutional Law No. 19-FZ. On the Perpetuation of the Victory of the Soviet People in the Great Patriotic War of 1941–1945. Effective as of the official publication date. 19 May. www.kremlin.ru/acts/bank/7872.

(2012). Federal Constitutional Law No. 20-FZ. On Amendments to Certain Legislative Acts of the Russian Federation regarding the Regulation of the Activities of Non-profit Organizations Performing the Functions of a Foreign Agent. Effective as of the official publication date. 20 July. www.kremlin.ru/acts/bank/35748

(2014). Federal Constitutional Law No. 05-FZ. On Amendments to Certain Legislative Acts of the Russian Federation. Effective as of the official publication date. 5 May. www.kremlin.ru/acts/bank/38395.

(2018). Federal Constitutional Law No. 317-F3, On the Amendments to Articles 11 and 14 of the Federal Law 'On Education in the Russian Federation'. Effective as of the official publication date. 3 August. www.kremlin.ru/acts/bank/43466.

(2021). Federal Constitutional Law No. 01-FZ. On Amendments to the Federal Law 'On Perpetuating the Victory of the Soviet People in the Great Patriotic War of 1941–1945. Effective as of the official publication date. 7 July. www.kremlin.ru/acts/bank/46972.

(2022a). Federal Constitutional Law No. 32-F3. O vnesenii izmeneniy v Ugolovniy kodeks Rossiyskoy Federacii i stat'i 31 i 151 Ugolovno-processual'nogo kodeksa Rossiyskoy Federacii. Effective as of the official publication date. 3 April. http://publication.pravo.gov.ru/Document/View/0001202203040007.

(2022b). Federal Constitutional Law No. 255-F3. On Monitoring the Activities of Individuals under Foreign Influence. Effective as of the official publication date. 14 July. http://kremlin.ru/acts/bank/48170/page.

(2022c). Decree N. 809. Executive Order Approving the Fundamentals of State Policy for the Preservation and Strengthening of Traditional Russian Spiritual and Moral Values. Effective as of the official publication date. 9 November. www.kremlin.ru/acts/news/69810.

(2022d). Zapreschaetsya propaganda netradicionnykh seksual'nykh otnosheniy [Propaganda of Nontraditional Sexual Relations Is Prohibited]. *News of the State Duma of the Russian Federation*. 24 November. http://duma.gov.ru/news/55838.

Suny, Ronald Grigor. (2001). The Empire Strikes Out: Imperial Russia, 'National' Identity and Theories of Empire. In Suny, Ronald Grigor, et al., eds., *A State of Nations Empire and Nation-Making in the Age of Lenin and Stalin*. Oxford: Oxford University Press, pp. 23–66.

Surzha, Arseniy. (2021). Bolezn' ushla v noch' [Illness Went into the Night]. *Teatr*. 18 November. http://oteatre.info/bolezn-ushla-v-nos.

Teatr Naciy. https://theatreofnations.ru/en/pages/o-teatre.

Tlostanova, Madina. (2015). Can the Post-Soviet Think? On Coloniality of Knowledge, External Imperial and Double Colonial Difference. *Intersections*, 1:2, pp. 38–58.

(2019). Decolonial AestheSis and the Post-Soviet Art. *Afterall*, 48:1, pp. 100–7.

Wood, Elizabeth A. (2011). Performing Memory: Vladimir Putin and the Celebration of World War II in Russia. *Soviet and Post-Soviet Review*, 38:172–200.

Ugarov, Mikhail & Konstantin Shavlovskiy. (2007). Tochka nerazreshimosti [The Point of No Return]. *Seans*. 25 February. https://seance.ru/articles/tochka-nerazreshimosti.

Zhanaidarov, Olzhas. (2019). Svoy – chuzhoy [One's Own – Someone Else's]. Unpublished article.

Acknowledgements

This research is funded by the Social Sciences and Humanities Research Council of Canada (SSHRC). My gratitude goes to Trish Reid and Liz Tomlin, the co-editors of the series, and artists and journalists Zhenya Berkovich, Anastasia Patlay, Nana Grinstein, Olzhas Zhanaidarov, Zoe Ruter, Anton Khitrov, Varvara Sklez, Mikhail Kaluzhsky, Alla Shenderova, Kirill Serebrennikov, Anna Shalashova, Elena Koval'skaya, and Aleksey Bartoschevich. A special 'thank you' goes to Dmitri Priven and Alessandro Simari.

Cambridge Elements

Theatre, Performance and the Political

About the Series

Elements in Theatre, Performance and the Political showcases ground-breaking research that responds urgently and critically to the defining political concerns, and approaches, of our time. International in scope, the series engages with diverse performance histories and intellectual traditions, contesting established histories and providing new critical perspectives.

Cambridge Elements

Theatre, Performance and the Political

Elements in the Series

Theatre Revivals for the Anthropocene
Patrick Lonergan

Re-imagining Independence in Contemporary Greek Theatre and Performance
Philip Hager

Performing Nationalism in Russia
Yana Meerzon

A full series listing is available at: www.cambridge.org/ETPP

For EU product safety concerns, contact us at Calle de José Abascal, 56–1°, 28003 Madrid, Spain or eugpsr@cambridge.org.

www.ingramcontent.com/pod-product-compliance
Ingram Content Group UK Ltd.
Pitfield, Milton Keynes, MK11 3LW, UK
UKHW022146080726
473066UK00010B/787

* 9 7 8 1 0 0 9 4 5 1 9 6 3 *